COUNTRY NEIGHBOURS

Also available in this series:

Fred Archer	BENEDICT'S POOL
Peter Austen	THE COUNTRY ANTIQUE DEALER
Mary Barnard	THE DIARY OF AN OPTIMIST
Pip Beck	A WAAF IN BOMBER COMMAND
Adrian Bell	THE CHERRY TREE
Mary Sydney Burke	THE SOLDIER'S WIFE
Jennifer Davies	TALES OF THE OLD GYPSIES
Roger Hutchings	CRYSTAL PALACE VISTAS
Ken Hankins	A CHILD OF THE THIRTIES
Herbert C. Harrison	THE MILL HOUSE AND THEREABOUTS
Gregory Holyoake	THE PREFAB KID
Erma Harvey James	WITH MAGIC IN MY EYES
Joy Lakeman	THEM DAYS
Len Langrick	SNOWBALL: GO FIND YOURSELF A SCHOOL
Florence Mary McDowell	OTHER DAYS AROUND ME
Madeline MacDonald	THE LAST YEAR OF THE GANG
Angela Mack	DANCING ON THE WAVES
Brian P. Martin	TALES FROM THE COUNTRY PUB
Roger Mason	GRANNY'S VILLAGE
Cicely Mayhew	BEADS ON A STRING
Christian Miller	A CHILDHOOD IN SCOTLAND
Katharine Moore	QUEEN VICTORIA IS VERY ILL
J. C. Morten	I REMAIN, YOUR SON JACK
and Sheila Morten	
Pauline Neville	PEGGY
Humphrey Phelps	JUST ACROSS THE FIELDS
Angela Raby	THE FORGOTTEN SERVICE
Phyl Surman	PRIDE OF THE MORNING
Doreen Louie West	LOUIE: AN OXFORD LADY
Elizabeth West	HOVEL IN THE HILLS
Hazel Wheeler	HALF A POUND OF TUPPENNY RICE
William Woodrow	ANOTHER TIME, ANOTHER PLACE

Country Neighbours

David Green

ISIS
LARGE PRINT
Oxford

First published in Great Britain 1948
by Blandford Press

The publisher has made all efforts to trace the owner of the work without success, and would be pleased to hear from the Author's estate.

British Library Cataloguing in Publication Data
Green, David, 1910-
  Country neighbours. – Large print ed.
  1. Green, David, 1910-   –Homes and haunts – England –
  Oxfordshire 2. Country life – England – Oxfordshire
  3. Large type books 4. Church Hanborough (Oxfordshire,
  England) – Social life and customs – 20th century
  I. Title
  942.5'7'082'092

        ISBN 0-7531-9700-6 (hb)
        ISBN 0-7531-9701-4 (pb)

Printed and bound by Antony Rowe, Chippenham and Reading

CONTENTS

Introduction

Full Circle

A little measly talk over neighbours is right enough; it do make the day go by a little quicker, and sends a body to bed with a chuckle.

MRS. ELLIS's *"Villager"*

INTRODUCTION

Neighbours are not chosen, and in ours we have been lucky, both in the Cotswolds and here, some eight miles from Oxford, where we live in a small stone cottage beside the church.

In the essays that follow I have tried to do something towards sharing this good fortune, though none knows better than he who has attempted such a record how easy it is to kill your characters with a notebook, how hard to bring 'em back alive.

"All the right country conversation," writes Edmund Blunden in his delightful "English Villages," "is too subtle and involved in circumstance to yield to analysis, or rise up in its fullness from a record . . ." Cadence, facial expression, gesture are bound to escape, to say nothing of "atmosphere" (the life of hut, cottage, mill, or wherever it is that your subject has his being).

Even so, some characters — we have all met them — are so rich and concentrated that even when doubly distilled in ink, sufficient of their essence may yet come through to make the attempt worth while. Shall I ever forget dashing in after that walk with Ellen (p. 129) and without stopping to kick off wellingtons typing fast for half an hour, in a desperate race with memory, to get down every word she had said and to have some sort of detailed record of the shabby, exotic, charming little creature she was? Fresh in the mind, too, is the diffidence of that Cornish violet grower (p. 214), a natural poet, about his "foreign" way of speaking. "Sometimes we have to correct ourselves to show you what we mean," he said, after some little misunderstanding about a fuchsia fence and a stone hedge, "we've got to try to improve things to get you to understand what we say." "For heaven's sake," said I, "do nothing of the kind. I can follow you very well." (Far better, I might have added, than that shepherd friend of mine (p. 73) who on occasion must needs check his "Fieldtown talk" and "put it up together a bit rounder" if I am to understand what his racy Cotswold yarns are about.)

The scene of most of the book is laid between the rivers Windrush and Evenlode, in that elm and willow country lying north-west of Oxford. The fact, then, that my theme and thread twists and winds about and doubles back on itself may be due in part to river influence; and in part to rural material which, like most characterful countrymen, declines to be drilled into a neat pattern or made to conform to rules which fail to find in the country the same awed respect and slavish observance as in the town.

He to whom Mr. Blunden refers as "the anonymous artisan of the English village" plays a more prominent part here than squire, doctor, parson, schoolmaster or even farmer, these good people having written and been written about so much. The women too are not, technically speaking, ladies-of-the-manor, though in a more general sense they most certainly are. I sometimes think that, as a friend once wrote to me from the Cotswolds, "the highest form of civilisation is to be found among old ladies, especially those who have had large families and seen them grow up, and know everything and now sit back and watch." Assuredly one had that feeling in the quiet presence of old Mrs. Chick and Mrs. Strawberry Jim.

Perhaps it is coincidence that, except for one or two passages concerned with children, the average age of those who have found their way into this book is high. Does it smack of decadence that one should find their talk, more often than not, livelier than that of the young and even the not-so- young? I wonder. There is more to it than their having more to look back on, these oldsters, or than their being more mature and able to give eye-witness accounts of the days of our grandparents. To those I have in mind there is a tang, a saltiness that comes of their way of living and believing, a rich way of seeing and storing things (like wine in the wood) and so of expressing them . . . We take these old people so much for granted, yet is not the type in its entirety — stability, ruggedness of character and all — fast dying out and are we not all too soon going to find that the musk has lost its scent and the salt its savour?

Turn then to those still very much with us: Strawberry Jim parting the leaves to show his "lovely fruit." . . . Tom Sermon all but hidden, in his home-made greenhouse, by great trusses of tomatoes . . . Johnny Horne straightening up from some particularly arduous job on his bee-loud acre. "Hope they don't make me a gardener in the next world though," he says, treating me to his water-melon grin, "I get more than enough of it here." "You'll be far too much in demand among the dukes and earls and viscounts as gentleman's gentleman," I assure him, "their ghosts will be jostling each other for you, you'll see." He laughs. "Yes, '*Now* we'll be all right,' I guess they'll be saying, '*now* we'll be well looked after, now they've let in old Horne.'" . . .

And now to all these good and tolerant friends, all who have so good-humouredly helped to make this book, I would say thank you. What there is of yourselves in it I know to be good, however amateurishly I may have played producer. What there is of the author (in Chapter Three, for instance) may easily be skipped in favour of the more entertaining people — ex-butler, nurseryman, miller — whose stories have been kept till the last.

Thanks, too, to *Country Life* for permission to reprint "Strawberry Jim's Story," "Blenheim Fifty Years Ago," the account of our incident with the tawny owl (p. 148) and notes on the Earl of Rochester at High Lodge; to the *Manchester Guardian* for similar kindness regarding our "Caravan Neighbour" and "Anglo-Roman Interlude"; and to *The Countryman* for, among much else, my opening quotation and for allowing reproduction of "Bells" (p. 104) and the poems "Monday Morning on the Common" and "Evolution of a Dryad" by the author's wife, Joyce Margaret Westrup, referred to in these pages as J, to whom the book is affectionately dedicated. Thank you one and all.

D. B. G.

CHAPTER
ONE

Above the Windrush

(1) STRAWBERRY JIM'S STORY

It is two o'clock of a hot, still, Cotswold afternoon.
The rush of the record strawberry harvest is just over,
and so, with an ache in the back but with mind well at
ease, the village perched above the Windrush sleeps in
the sun. The door of my friend Strawberry Jim's
cottage is open, and quietly, my shoes following the
shallow channel worn in the flagstones, I walk in.

On either side of the parlour window, which frames
a vast green landscape of wooded hills and water
meadows, Mr. and Mrs. Strawberry Jim are asleep.
This is awkward. Twenty hot miles I have cycled to see
them, my time is short, and now, as I look at them,
there seems nothing to prevent their sleeping till
Domesday.

I tiptoe out into the sun and stroll up to the cottage-
sized church where from a beam inside the porch a
nesting swallow looks enquiringly down. It was here
seven years ago that Strawberry Jim, almost
unrecognizable in best brown suit, led my bride
between flowering grasses and up the strawberry-
scented aisle (for no one had ever seen or smelt so

1

many strawberries as then filled the church) and gave her away . . . But that's another story.

To-day, if he ever wakes, I mean to get Jim to tell me once more the story of the Venture, of how he founded an industry, changed the lives of his neighbours and brought prosperity to every cottage in the village.

Strawberry Jim (you will see how he earned the name) is 84, his wife a year older. He was born in this cottage, has worn it threadbare, like a favourite old jacket — he often talks of discarding it but never will. His quiet voice, when at last he rouses, makes little more sound than did his breathing when asleep. Indeed, his talk is like dreams, drifting from one scene to another, from farmers who "think theirselves big 'uns till they come up against we" to the pedigree Jerseys he has pastured in an obliging neighbour's field. "I lets 'er know they was a-comin', see, and I never hears nothin' further." "Some people are very unbusinesslike," I sympathize. But "Ah no. When I heard nothin', see, I know'd as it was all right and I sent they heifers along."

Gently, trying hard to reduce my tempo — at least a generation too fast — to his, I coax him round to the tale I like best, the story of the labourer who, forty-five years ago, dared to be different and plant raspberries and strawberries on those windswept hillside allotments, more than 700 feet up. I picture the strain on Jim's trousers as he bends to speak to the earth and I see behind him, leaning on a gate, the norfolk-jacketed figure of a Victorian squire, watching in silence. Now Jim straightens up and the watcher hails him. "What be up to, Jim," he shouts (so Jim tells us), "plantin' them bits o' things there?" "I told him what my business was," says Jim, "experimentin' like, a-plantin' out raspberries as'd done s'well in the gyarden. Eighteen shillin' they'd brought us . . . The only work to be had those times was farmer's work, ah, and poorish at that, ten shillin' a week it come to, or p'raps eleven, so summat had to be done."

And then the sequel. Better plants from the squire's walled garden in the valley, Royal Sovereign strawberries which "only came out last year." The squire himself helps to plant them and slips Jim half a crown to drink his health at the end of the day. "So I kep' on," says Jim, "and planted a smartish bit, strawberries and canes and it paid well." He soon had his first acre under soft fruit which, in his third year of farming, yielded £300. This, of course, was a fortune, and every savable penny was pounced on by his thrifty wife and banked.

But indeed I had almost forgotten her, sitting quietly there, till a soft voice said, "And what did I do? Didn't I do nothin'?" Jim was not abashed. "Her built the shed," he said. "Ah, and the floor of the stable when we come to need 'un. Handed 'er the stwuns, didn't I, and her fitted 'em in." I said something about this being a skilled-job and how then could she have known the way to set about it. "Well," said Jim seriously, "there's that likeness o' me on the wall there, look at it now." I looked at the huge familiar framed photograph of the youthful Jim in which he wears a proud look never seen on the man we know and with it, perhaps the cause of it, a breeches suit of Victorian whipcord so tight, you would say it were madness for the occupant to attempt to cross his legs. Yet there they are, triumphantly crossed as too are the arms; and the seams, as far as one can tell, still hold. "Her made them clothes," said Jim simply. "Ah, wonderful her was that way, at tailorin' and such; folks come from miles." So *that* was how, with skilled fitter's fingers, the stable floor came to be laid.

"I was never so happy," Jim went on, "as workin' like I was then, without a master, and very soon I had the mastery o' the job. Folks said they never see such strawberries and some o' the rasps was as big as that egg-cup there," nodding to a generous-looking egg-cup on top of the American organ. "And yet folks was still makin' sport at me when I was a-plantin' o' them. Ah, there was one chap I mind particular," he said, warming to his theme, "stood up in the Council 'e did, when we was a-wantin' to grow more fruit for the village, and 'Gentlemen' 'e says, 'gentlemen, is it right for anyone to grow strawberries in a open field and encourage our boys to steal? Gentlemen,' 'e says, 'mark my words now, strawberries is not cabbages,' 'e says ah, just like that, 'strawberries is not cabbages.' Then I spoke up. 'No,' says I, 'and any fool knows they byent.' And the chairman 'e says, 'You keep right on, Jim, for you've a right to grow just what you've a mind.'"

For fifteen years, such is rural conservatism and such was lack of cash, in spite of unfailing and unconcealed success, Strawberry Jim and his nephew continued to be the only strawberry growers in the village. Meanwhile

4

the allotments adjoining Jim's became so neglected that the Council asked him to take the whole lot over and this he did, "or we should all 'a bin turned out." To-day, of course, every square foot of that land and of the surrounding fields — in all about 20 acres farmed by some eighteen growers — produces strawberries (raspberries, as too subject to disease, have been dropped), and for the fair distribution of plots and plants and indeed for every kind of expert help and advice Jim himself has been mainly responsible. "Women and all," he says, chuckling, "they goes at it red hot to get their bit o' money. Last year a woman told me she turned £60 off about half a chain." In some cases even vegetables for the pot have been crowded out and have to be bought from less strawberry-minded neighbours.

It is surely to his credit that Jim has never discouraged competition. On the contrary, with one farmer especially, he was insistent that he should become a grower, visiting him when worry over farm losses had driven the poor man to his bed, offering his help and telling him, "If you don't get out o' this, it'll kill ee, you know." "I don't believe," said the anxious farmer, "if I was squared up to-day I'd be worth tuppence." But thanks to Jim he did rouse himself and take Jim's advice, tottered out "with 'is coat collar up, I remember s'well" to plan his land afresh and ultimately "did well with strawberries, out and out well, best job he ever 'ad. Growed fine stuff too, wonderful crops . . . Ah, and the rest o' the folks done well too, thorough well, more than they expected."

"A workin' man as lives in the village," Jim explains, "someone as we can trust, we be always willin' to help out. But strangers, comin' and beatin' us p'raps at parish meetin' — no, we watches them. Had enough o' that years ago. Very near got to fightin' in church too, for that's where we had to meet those days, and we couldn't master 'un, no more than about by one. It learnt us to make sure of a majority, see, and that meant goin' round and countin' up our lot afore we went in. Ah, a hard scramble that was," and then with a reflective twinkle, "Ah, we be some chaps."

As for marketing, it seems it was never a problem. For the first few years Jim's crop was disposed of at local shops or at Cheltenham market. Later he bought a horse and waggon, a quiet, patient, rich chestnut horse and a little blue waggon that came to be known and welcomed for miles around — at Burford, Stow-on-the-Wold, Northleach, the Rissingtons, the Slaughters, and Bourton-on-the-Water. The hamlet of Northleach came in for special attention, being warned in advance of his visitations so that the town crier might be tipped a shilling and encouraged to go his way in the market-place crying "Strawberries! Strawberries for sale!" and of course what o'clock to expect them. "I got used to the folks," Jim says, "and they got used to me." The only wrinkle on these occasions was the pretty girl who held the bridle while Jim was selling and bartering in Northleach's multitudinous pubs. Almost invariably, when Jim at last returned to the waggon, the girl who, as I said, was pretty, had vanished; till at last Jim could stand it no longer and dismissed the young hussy in favour of a kinswoman of his own. Plain and not young, I supposed; but not a bit of it. "Her was handsome enough," reflected Jim, "ah, and flighty too, given the chance. But her was a relation, see, and 'er knew I could beat 'er."

The strawberry fields themselves are mostly on the east side of the hill, very exposed, but out of the way of most frosts and "wonderful good for soft fruit." Few farmers, I imagine, would be reassured to know that their land was "brashy, gets very tight, blows up cuts, gets sour and ploughs up raw," yet this is how Jim describes the soil which year after year produces magnificently generous crops. "It's all very nice sweet land though," he adds amelioratingly, "s'light, you see, and all of it grows strawberries well."

The berries that do best here are Royal Sovereign, Oxleys and Paxtons, and to these bountiful berries must go the credit for the amazing contribution from this once poverty stricken village of just over eighty souls (including children) of £1,500 to a wartime savings campaign. "I don't suppose there's one in the village as didn't put a bit in," says Jim proudly, "beat all the villages round, we did, and one of 'em five times bigger than we." On the village's declining birthrate, however, Jim is gloomy. "Folks ain't 'ad the youngsters like they used to," he explains carefully, "Well now, that counts up. We be running back now again to eighty. Well over a hundred we used to be," and such throngs of children blocking his way as he came laden with glistening baskets from the fields that a toll of a berry per mouth had to be paid before he could get by them, yes, and sometimes money too, for knowing as you did that from a father's wage packet of ten shillings some of them must be 'benefiting' by less than a shilling a week, "you couldn't refuse them."

With all the fruit to see to — planting, weeding, strawing, picking, and that most necessary job, bird-scaring, performed by frequent tugs at long necklaces of empty tins strung above the rows — you might have thought that the Strawberry Jims had their hands full enough. But at the time he tells of (some forty years ago) there was no post office in the village, not even a shop unless you counted the old woman who sold "black jumbles, home-made 'uns, in that corner 'ousen over there." The pony-and-trap postie used to bring the mail at midday and sit in the church porch "having his dinner," to give folks a chance of answering their letters and bringing them along without, no doubt, interrupting his afternoon nap.

Several council meetings were held before some bold spirit found voice to own that he had been "thinkin' of James's wife down there" as potential post-mistress. A show of hands, a little heavy correspondence and the job was hers. This, of course, meant a lot of bother and responsibility, for even the new-fangled telephone came to be installed. However, looking on the bright side, it meant all told an extra shilling a week, and in those days, as Jim says, "you could buy a nice bit with it anyhow, if you worked it right." As time went on, Jim tells us, "we got to two shillin' and kep' gradually risin' till now it's a pound a week.

8

But you would never guess now, as you walked between the strewed rows in the high fields or between the pews of what H. J. Massingham calls the "pigmy, ex-Norman church" that here not so long ago were scenes of wrangle. Yet a "terrible hard scuffle" the growers had to get their way in the teeth of farmers who were for ever telling them they had "too much land." But the growers stood their ground, and it is thanks to their staunchness, and of course to Jim's enterprise and good heart, that the village is now the most prosperous for miles. "There is nobody poor in the village," asserts Jim, "I don't know one. And I'll tell you another thing. The shopkeepers say they can always tell when pickin's begun because for miles around the pickers be all a-payin' their bills."

So once more I left him with his strong handshake and with a message for a mutual friend. "Tell 'er," he said, "we lacks for nothin'. Sense p'raps, but not food nor money nor nothin' . . . and tell 'er I be savin' a nice bit o' pig for when she comes."

(II) THE OTHER STORY

When we think, as we often do, of the Strawberry Jims, it seems to us that we have known them always. Certainly, up in that hilltop village of theirs one is less conscious of time than anywhere else. It was only when we were back in the world of business (for at that time we were both working on a country magazine) that the contrast in pace came home to us and wellnigh stunned us.

When the pressure of work at the office was heaviest, or so it always seemed, a bell would ring and snatching the telephone J would hear — silence, and then in the slowest possible Cotswold drawl, "Is that you, J-i-i-ice . . . how b'ist getten a-a-an?" And indeed what need had Jim to hurry? At his plodding pace he had done more useful work than we in our feverish ways were ever likely to do.

I once rashly asked a Cotswold shepherd when he was expecting his first lambs. (I have since learnt that wise and superstitious shepherds expect nothing and that some prefer not to count the lambs when they arrive.) He was, of course, non-committal. "When the time comes," he said fatalistically, "that's it." It was just so with our friend the strawberry-grower. The fruit lying in the sun on his high fields was not to be hurried. No more was he.

The pace up there was gentle, as were the people we knew; and there was continuity. Always when we stepped into Jim's cottage, after crossing the Windrush and walking between clouds of blue cranesbill up the precipitous Old Lane, no matter if it were the first visit for months, we were made to feel that we had never been away.

"I be glad you come," he would say, "we was just thinkin' of you," while his smiling, white-haired wife (Jim himself was her coiffeur), without a word reached up to the corner cupboard where the tea caddy was kept.

Over the teacups (the milk, by the way, was tinned: they distrusted their neighbour's cow) talk would be village talk, and, for one of us at least, difficult to follow. How, J enquired, was Young Jim's Aida and was Mrs. Strawberry Jim's knitting going to be for hers? Doing nicely, she was, and Jim only wished he could say the same for "our Snowdrop." Ah, it'd take a smartish bit o'vettin' to get Snowdrop back to her normal yield. From there we might drift to the "Jackie-Bo-Peep's nest" he had found beside the Old Lane or the "nice bit o'mate" Jim had (and he pressed us to share it with him) for next day's dinner.

But in a small cottage such as theirs, housing shop, post-office and "private" dwelling all within an area of about four penny stamps, conversation in the parlour was bound to be interrupted. One would be sidetracked by low-pitched demands for Woodbines and high-pitched entreaties for sherbert dabs; or it might be elegant Mrs. Sprightly calling to telephone.

It was this same Mrs. Sprightly, Jim would repeatedly tell his wondering audience, who had presented herself at the shop one summer's afternoon, "na-ked as a ro-bin" and had then, without a blush or any sort of apology or explanation, called for a bottle of ginger-pop. It was a story we never managed to fathom, though we supposed she must have been "dressed" in some slight kind of sun-suit; but there was no doubt that the incident had made its mark and that it always cheered our old friend to tell of it.

Keeping open house as the Jims did, on Sundays as well as weekdays, meant that the shop also was never closed; though I suppose those used to town shops might say that this one never seemed fully open. One

11

harvest Sunday, when trade was so brisk that Jim couldn't settle to his smoke, J volunteered to keep shop for him, and as far as we in the parlour could tell, managed well enough, in spite of the fact that soon after she had taken over there was such an influx of custom as Jim had not known for years. "Quite a run on the peppermints," murmured J leaving the shop to get ready for church.

Later, as we were singing "We plough the fields and scatter," it began to dawn on some of us what J's shopkeeping had meant. At every noise-laden breath overpowering wafts of peppermint swept round the little church. It had not, of course, been her intention to serve the village with more than twice its moneysworth of bullseyes, but there it was, the miscalculation made, the news had run through the village as fast as young legs could carry it till not a sweet tooth in the parish but knew "Miss Westrup" was keeping shop — and how she was keeping it. Presto! The cupboard shoplet was besieged; and how serve one wideawake customer with less than his or her neighbour? Never, I guessed, were hearts more unfeignedly thankful. Never could incense have smelt more strongly of mint.

There were, of course, no strawberries in the church for Harvest, but in one memory at least the crop gleamed brightly, and once again Strawberry Jim, we noticed, had given thanks in his characteristic way. His best vegetables were there as a matter of course, as were the three fat red roses in the lectern (a hen's egg hidden behind each) from his wife's flower garden. But all this was not enough. On an upturned milking-stool he had built and thatched, with astonishing neatness, a little round straw-brick, and stood it against a pale sandstone pillar, where it quite obviously belonged.

Why, at a festival of thanksgiving, we should have been treated to a sermon of violence I cannot say. Perhaps it was that the parson, knowing well that Harvest marks the only Sunday in the calendar when all villagers are churchgoers, was determined to win and hold their attention at all costs. However it was, he harangued us to such purpose that every peppermint was soon immobilised and left to melt as it would; and when three prize King Edwards (grown by Strawberry Jim and dislodged by emphasis) went bouncing and thumping down the pulpit stairs, there was barely a titter. In the battle raging above they were, we felt, so much spent shot, while the pulpit was manifestly a charger which at any moment might snort Ah-ha! Yet at last, having fought and stormed at us and triumphed, the rector reined in, spoke quietly, became human, even smiled. Why, what miserable sinners we all were, that smile seemed to say, and wasn't he one of us? The Great God of Battles was very well, we had just had a taste of him, but wasn't there a more comradely being, the god, in fact, of "Green Pastures," the same who, we would remember, smiled upon his children when he chanced on them innocuously a-junketing and, still smiling, gave as his commandment that gloriously plebeian edict: "Let the fish-fry proceed" . . . There, surely, was a god to understand a village. *There* was a god for a village to take to its heart.

It was this same rector who, replying to my letter asking him to marry us, so thoughtfully assured me that he would "keep me right, throughout the service, with whispers that could not be overheard."

When the great day came (July 2nd) I drove out to the village early to make sure that the little church was well banked with flowers. Remembering Harvest and how the village had then excelled itself, I now expected, as I pulled the heavy door and stepped down into the nave's cool whiteness, to be dazzled by roses and peonies and phloxes and carnations, "bells and flowerets of a thousand hues." . . . Instead, I was taken aback with dismay. A few wilting Canterbury bells rested limp heads against the pulpit, while at the pew ends drooping evergreens and garlands of ivy gave sharp reminder that in the midst of life we are in death. I rather fancy old Mr. Brontë would have liked it. I did not.

I turned to the cleaner-decorator, a large woman on her knees in the half-scrubbed aisle. She smiled. Yes, it did all look nice, didn't it? Though if it hadn't been for the fruit (the rush of a late strawberry harvest), it might have looked even better . . . I thanked her hollowly and looked at my watch.

Part of the bride's scheme had been the lavish use of strawberries, not merely as food but for church decoration. Part of the nightmare now was the mountain of glistening fruit given us by the Jims and waiting to be hulled (for guests couldn't be expected, the experts warned us, to deal with their own).

So it was that the bridegroom's mother, brother and sister-in-law, in wedding garb and without panic, squeezed themselves into the toy vestry and, cheerfully dyeing their hands carmine, stripped the berries; while the bridegroom ran down the Old Lane to the Windrush, to the water meadows where her favourites grew — loosestrife and water forget-me-not, bedstraw and knapweed, "button" scabious and giant burnet, the burnet bobbing about among the buttercups like spots before the eyes. Wildly I grabbed them, and sweating, glanced again at my watch: twenty minutes to go . . .

I thanked heaven that no one was by as I staggered up the green tunnel of the Old Lane, snatching bryony and willow-herb as I went, and ran panting into the post-office and called for jam pots. Then I flung down my jacket and nipped into the back kitchen where, at Mrs. Jim's direction, I found the biggest earthenware bread-crock I had ever seen. Into it went hogweed and fool's parsley from the roadside, and in a matter of seconds an "arrangement"of which a Bond Street florist might well have been proud.

Willow-herb hid the church stove. Bryony, with its glossy heart-shaped leaves, ousted the ivy; meadowsweet seemed to float over the altar; mixed bunches shone from sills and corners; and from everywhere else there gleamed baskets and baskets of distractingly fragrant strawberries. The three fat red roses in the lectern were, of course, from Mrs. Strawberry Jim.

It was just as in shirtsleeves I was returning slop pails (used for filling crocks) to the post-office that the first guests arrived, and as I fled I caught a glimpse of my richest uncle in his chauffeur'd car, the whole glistening equipage, womenfolk and all, *au dernier chic*. They saw me and quickly looked away.

By this time I was badly in need of a wash, but there was no running water at Jim's post-office and rather than run the gauntlet to the pump on the green I dipped into the bottle greenness of the rainwater butt, with the result that when the breathless bridegroom appeared in church his face was pale green. The church, however, looked and smelt glorious, and that seemed, at the moment, all that mattered.

From where I stood through the old diamond panes I could plainly see Strawberry Jim, the bride on his arm, walking slowly between the graves and the unscythed grasses. I was so very glad we had chosen him for the giving away . . .

Mrs. Strawberry Jim had been unable to persuade herself to church "with all them fine folks," but after the service, on a sudden and just as she was, coatless and coifless except for her halo of white hair, she climbed into the nearest car and in due course climbed out of it at our wide-swung farm gate. It was the first time she had been out of her village since she couldn't remember when and the ride had been nice and "they flowers down the hill" (cow parsley) very pretty. So many strangers all in Sunday best were a little bewildering, but once in the old house (early sixteenth-century) she was much more at home than they were. She did not think it "quaint" or have to be helped upstairs. She was up them and stroking a fur rug and exclaiming at the four-poster while others were vaguely seeking food downstairs and praying that the strawberries hadn't gone astray, which, of course, they had.

The crocks of flowers about the house she pronounced "a wonder" and having taken in everything, from the bellows beside the grate to the minute bed of heliotrope which was J's special pride, she hopped over the stile and crossed Back Orchard to our landlord's model farm, while Jim ran his eye over the farmer's new cowhouse and decided that for all those milking-machines and spotless overalls, he could "likely show them better butter back home."

When, a day or two later, we next visited the Strawberry Jims, we found Mrs. Jim vaguely searching for a bread-crock. So large it had been and her cottage so small and yet now the great crock was nowhere to be found. It was all a bit worrying. I ran to the church and retrieved it and she brightened at once. Jim, she told us, was "up the Council." "And shall we give him your love?" J called to her as we set out to meet him. "Reckon he's got that already, hasn't 'a?" she called back.

It was a clear day in November when I last cycled over to the post-office cottage and I found Jim alone. But I may as well quote the entry I made at the time.

Jim was having a haircut in preparation for to-morrow's journey — *in a henhouse on a lorry* — to the Forest of Dean, where Mrs. Jim, who has been poorly, is wintering with her daughter. He had been immensely pleased with the Strawberry Jim article in *Country Life* (pp. 1 to 9). "Never knew a book so praised up. Folks fell in love with it," so that he couldn't keep his copy or find out where they had sent it on. I promised to send another. Everyone, he said, asked if he had written it, and so on. "But there was a lot more I coulda told you, David," he said, "ah, and good stuff, too, if I'd 'a given it thought."

We talked and then, seemingly on a sudden impulse, he showed me upstairs, pointing out as we went the dangling, ragged piece of stair-carpet that had tripped him so badly months ago. "I'm better of it now." So tough! And the carpet still not mended!!

Arrived at an immense painted wardrobe, he slowly opened every one of its doors and drawers. From one drawer he pulled out a little old black bowler and put it on. "Haven't worn it more'n two-three times ever, shouldn't think, but still up-to-date, isn't 'a? Quite a toff in it too, byain't I?" He put it back and shut all up again and showed me two "convenient chairs" (commodes), demonstrating them by lifting seats, and a bed with a number of waterproofs on it "to keep the wet out," having lately had serious trouble with the roof. He then unearthed a huge framed photograph of two cows in a gloomy field. "Ah, them was ours, them two. They was never black though. Come out black in the photograph." He was as always full of welcome and twinkle and fond messages.

Yes, it's far too long since we saw him and high time we took that little rough yellow road again, the switchback road that runs between banks of blue cranesbill and follows the Windrush.

(III) NOSTALGIC JOURNEY

When the railway company lost my bicycle and bought me a utility one I did not care for, everyone was most helpful. "What you want is a sports model," they said, "get you places in no time. I got the very thing."

I was almost ashamed to own that it was not one of those rakish bend-you-doubles that I had in mind, although of course for the serious cyclist who likes to keep his eye on the road and his chin on his knees, nothing could be better. No, what I wanted was what manufacturers call a "Tourist," and a very proper appellation too, a tour being (so my dictionary tells me) "a rambling excursion; a short journey for pleasure; a roving journey, *including stops at various places.*" Which reminds me of the time when I heard a child ask, as we were admiring the view, "Mummy, why have they stopped?"

It seemed futile to try to explain my preference for travelling hopefully, even haltingly, rather than this grim business of arriving in no time, with curvature of the spine. Baldly then I owned to my quaint, archaic taste; and "Oh," said they indulgently, "you mean a proper old sit-up-and-beg."

And a proper old sit-up-and-beg it is, even to a basket roomy enough for a fair-sized cabbage, even to a second "occasional" saddle for a small boy, even to an anti-theft device which, if you should be foolhardy enough to use and forget it, would neatly spill you on to the road at the first bend.

What I particularly like about it is that, unlike my "utility," it is characterful without being temperamental;

and further that, thanks to the village bicycleman, our able friend Frank Mason, who remade the thing for me, it is silent and boosts me sufficiently to see over hedges and spot the elegant plover brooding her eggs.

("Now, how much will that be altogether, Mr. Mason?" you ask. "Oh, about fourpence," he will tell you, or "About nine pence" or for a major repair to a mower, perhaps, "About one and six . . . I won't charge you much as it's holiday time.")

To-day — a hot, hazy day from an old-fashioned summer — I let my sit-up-and-beg take me across the Windrush at Burford and most of the way up the long hill beyond before stopping at a high grassy place where we used to find bee orchis.

It is years since I saw this place, though often, especially at dreary times during the war, I have had it in mind. It is hardly the conventional beauty spot, being, in fact, a ditch beside a main road, but it is a long wide ditch with a south bank to it where I have found the tree-pipit nesting, and for flowers it grows not only the common knapweeds, scabiouses, mallows, etc., typical of the Cotswold verges, but mats of thyme, yellow rockrose and milkwort, several vetches (including horseshoe and purple milk) and the deep blue cluster-bell (*Campanula glomerata*) which I have seen too seldom and never more manifestly at home. Added to all this, it is a ditch much frequented by burnet moths and marbled white butterflies. In short: a typical bee orchis locality.

Here and there the fine grasses have been flattened by trippers, but amazingly the bee orchis has not only survived but multiplied, so that once you have spotted it (not easy), you see the mauve wings and tawny "bees" everywhere. What is more, the pyramidal orchis has spread from its patch half a mile off and now adds to the blues and yellows, mauves and velvet-browns its own distinctive pink, which Johns calls "deep rose-coloured."

With the comfortable thought that perhaps our old haunts have not been spoiled and "our pleasant things laid waste" after all, I ride on to the lonely inn where I lived for three years.

Not much visible change here, though I know that the house is in different hands. The brass knocker shines cheerfully, "my" bedroom window is as it always was, wide open; and just outside it the same badly-lettered sign swings from the beam from which, one winter's night, a mysterious bird sang a loud and persistent reeling "song," which woke me and kept me awake, so that I felt bound to report it to *Country Life*.

But it was a mistake to follow the path at the back of the inn, the path that used to take us down to the fir wood. In the old days the high brambles down there had been a favourite nesting-place for bullfinch and blackcap, while in the wood itself there were goldcrests and wild strawberries, a great tit that built in an elder-stump underground, a robin's nest in a bank of bluebells . . . And how quiet it was, the quietest of many quiet places we knew, so that when the goldcrest sang we could hear each separate note . . . And the way the light came through the larches and the delicate grass grew greener than anywhere else. Wasn't it there

21

that we found hidden in a piece of rough sandstone that crisply-coiled ammonite? And wasn't it just there that we loosed the rescued fox-cub (she had been dug out and "tamed") and saw her dash off through the brambles towards Tangley, that lichened farm once famed for robbers and more latterly as the setting for "Lady into Fox"?

To-day there is no wood, none at all. With tractors and chains and all that makes this type of destruction easy it has been tidied up. All that remains is a stump or two, already overgrown with weeds and elder. It is nothing like so beautiful, but it is still quiet, even quieter. Not a bird sings.

I climb the path again and take another, along a steep wooded bank where J found white helleborine; and yes, the orchis persists, though not abundantly. It feels strange indeed to be climbing the little hill among the larches to the quarry we knew as "the camp." The meals we had there — buttered crumpets with watercress; chippolata and mushrooms; eggs, apples and tomatoes, and good strong Indian tea — the talks, the silences . . . And now? Thanks to a landslide and to the natural vigour of elder and nettles, the fireplace and the stone seat before it have disappeared, but man has not touched the place. The high larches are still there, and the smooth beeches, even to their roots, which reach down the side of the quarry and with ivy hide the rabbit-holes where we used to leave the food and the billycan before setting off to bathe.

"Do nip down to the mill and have a bathe," my companion of those days (and, when duty allows, of these) had urged me this morning, "I would love to hear how it is. I expect it's exactly the same. Some places are."

But the nipping is not easy. There is a vast rash of aerodrome, with its acre upon acre of obsolete planes, to circumnavigate, and further on, oats growing patchily over the once well-defined footpath, and blackthorn flourishing all round the field's edge.

The bicycle bucks and shies at the blackthorn and wants to turn back, but remembering what we have just been through I realize that "returning were as tedious as go o'er," and insist to the point of brutality. A puncture seems inevitable, when suddenly there we are at the sandy track which runs down between the ruined mill-house and its barn. The one perfect mullion, looking out over the Windrush and Snipe Meadow, still stands, drip-stone and all, though the pigeon's nest on the sill has given way to a vigorous briar which sends roses spraying over the top of the pale grey wall. All, at first glance at least, is very well.

As I come within sight of the river itself, where it flows under the small grey bridge and into the pool, I see that the log hut — Lord S's fishing hut — is still there, though it has lost its door and shutters and its air of being well-cared for. It has had its own little war, I guess. It is no longer the immaculate plaything I watched being thatched and afterwards used for polite fishing parties by fisher-lords and fisher-ladies. But it is not empty. Tucked into a corner of the straw roof there is a neat wren's nest, whence now whirrs the sitter, giving me a loud, scolding "Chrrrip!" as she goes by. I

23

see her out of the doorway and across the river before gently exploring the nest with my finger. (Years ago it was easy enough to count the smallest eggs, but now two or more get touched at the same time.) There seem to be any number of eggs, lying on brown hen's feathers and beginning to pile up against the feathered walls.

Nor is the wren the hut's only frequenter. The floor, white with droppings and dotted about with large grey pellets, speaks of owl. And how much, I wonder, does the wren mind him; or is there a mutual understanding about live-and-let-live and Ancient Lights?

So wondering I undress and slip into the river, letting the current carry me round the pool, as of old; and taking in each familiar tree and bush and plant as I go. At the very edge of the hut bank I recognize blue skull-cap and creeping Jenny, and on the other side there are, as there always were, meadow-sweet and blue cranesbill, loosestrife and willow-herb massed around that pollard willow which was the first thing one used to blink at after a long lie in the sun. The yellow loosestrife has gone, but over there by the wattle fence is the high willow Peter climbed, dripping river water, and there is the slippery place where he encouraged Tangley, the sheep-dog, to fall in. This may bush that leans down as though to screen the shallows. Ah, the may bush . . .

We had cycled some thirty stiff miles from Stratford-on-Avon, and, stifling day that it was, made straight as a kingfisher for the pool. It was no time for giving thought to correct river wear. We had no bathing things with us but, there being no one within sight or sound, we both slipped gratefully in, J in the rather thinly-screened shallows, myself in the deep pool, nearer bridge and hut.

We had just begun to wallow in the coolness — she in her small corner, I in mine — when out sprang a keeper who, addressing the only face visible, asked if it didn't know that this was one of Lord S's Very Private Places. Well yes, I admitted, I did, but surely Lord S. wouldn't mind? (I happened to know that he was tolerant, but so stern was my interrogator, I felt like Adam brought to book.) Not MIND? . . . The man — who looked to me overdressed from polished boots and gaiters upwards — made the most of his advantage, enlarging upon the enormity of swimming in any trout pool and especially in a pool belonging to his lord and above all in one of his lordship's Very Private Places . . .

At long last came a voice from behind the may bush: "Won't that man *ever* go away?" He heard and started a little, but was not to be hurried. He was young and probably human in spite of the polished gaiters, and inquisitive. Besides, he had more to say. But nothing lasts, not even the longest sermon, and there came a time when, thorough as he was, it must have seemed to him that he had done his full duty and that it might perhaps be as well to go. He went. And so, a few minutes later, did we — to Mrs. Bullfinch's at Great Rissington where, in those days of plenty, we could be sure of fresh cucumber sandwiches, to be consumed on the premises, beside a tall row of sweet peas.

25

There is no sign of a keeper now, as I grip tussocks of grass overhanging the bank and haul myself out. The only sounds are a sedge-warbler's song and an occasional glup-glup from under the bridge. Clearing a small patch of nettles I sit on the hut's warm brick step and take one of the owl-pellets carefully to pieces. It is almost all grey fur mixed with the bones of mice, the minute jaws still holding the all but invisible teeth. There are also a few small feathers . . . CHRRRIP! There goes the wren again, her note alarmingly loud from inside the hut. I must get on, though I could stay dreaming for hours, as we used, leaving busy-ness to the bees in that patch of white clover. The smell of it all: the "unforgettable, unforgotten river smell." Why, even the flies seem mannerly here and standoffish. And then the haze, that same silvery haze over willow and cranesbill and meadowsweet; and the timelessness; and the peace . . . CHRRRIP! I must go.

The way leads across the turfy field where I once found a flint from the Stone Age. It was lying beside a molehill, on a small sandy patch which made it look the foreigner it was. It had been sliced and pointed with enough deftness to leave a handy little groove for the thumb. "About 2,000 B.C.," the British Museum told me, "edge slightly used."

Then up the rough track and on to Strawberry Jim's. But there I am in for a shock. Mrs. Jim has fallen in the garden and broken her right arm. She goes into hospital to-night. For many months now she has been in a kind of tranquil second-childhood, recognizing almost no one except Jim, and yet able to enjoy the sunshine and her flowers which still persist although she has long since lost the skill to tend them. Not an unfitting evening, as we thought, to her long, hard day; for she is 86, was married at sixteen (he was seventeen), bore several children and worked at her post office as well as at her house and plot. Her little "pecked piece" of garden — each bed blue-bound with speedwell, as it used to be — is perched above the lane and only to be reached by a steep flight of stone steps.

"Her was a-pickin' flowers in the gyarden," Jim slowly explains, "looks safe enough, so I comes in here a minute and lights a cigarette. Then I hears a scuffle and g's out and there she is lyin' at the foot o' them steps, ah, flowers still in her two hands. I know just how it musta bin. Lookin' at her flowers, see, and wasn't a-takin' notice o' where she was steppin'."

He leads the way upstairs to where she lies on the big brass-knobbed bed, and I put J's pink sweet-williams into her shrivelled brown hand. She does not know me, but when the name of the giver is spoken her eyes light up. "She'll be comin' soon," Jim, tells her, "ah, and we'll likely be goin' over to see her flowers, both of us, soon as you're fit an' well." "I likes the sound o' that," she says.

But how one wishes at such times for the gift of comfortable words! As it is, nothing but the trite and the conventional will come; and so the flowers must speak for us both. I kiss her and go. Nor to Jim, in his worry and unhappiness, can I say what I would like to. J is the one. She will do far better, making his bed and

27

comforting him and going with him to the hospital. I must make for home now and tell her about it.

As I pass Jim's high fields I see his stalwart grandson busy hoeing and, leaving the bike, I confer with him about his "Gran", though for the present there is nothing more to be done. He offers me strawberries and together we begin to search the rough leaves of some rather well-picked rows. I enjoy strawberry-picking — who doesn't? — and think that I am doing well till he asks "How many?" "Nearly three," I say proudly. "Good," says he, "then I'll fill one more punnet and that'll make twelve pounds in all." . . .

"But how does he *do* it?" I ask as we hull the gleaming fruit at home.

"Oh, he was born to it. He used to be put down in his basket at the end of the rows while they picked, and I shouldn't wonder if he took in strawberry juice with his mother's milk. He's a credit to her, isn't he?"

He most certainly is.

CHAPTER TWO

Upper Evenlode Country

(I) TOWNSMAN TRIES TO TURN COUNTRYMAN
Intimately as I came to know the Strawberry Jims, I much doubt if, townsman as I was, I would ever have known them at all had I not first shared their welcome of J, whom they had long since accepted as one of themselves.

It is not easy for the town-bred young man, picking his way for the first time through the innocently smiling greenery of the countryside, to avoid all the uncharted bogs which, once he has become acclimatised and learnt the local topography and rules of behaviour (a long process), seem obvious enough.

As I call to mind the day I first came to live in the country, and see the green young man being directed by the lady of the manor to old Mrs. Frost's hilltop farm ("I do hope you're eccentric," said my guide, "it does so help the village through its long winter evenings"), I realize that it was just a question as to which of those bogs he fell into first. As it happened it was the one called FOOD.

It would have been difficult if not impossible to explain to Mrs. Frost why I could not bring myself to eat her nicely-cooked and served sheep's heart. It was not, as she seemed to think, that I distrusted all her farm food, nor yet that I was uncommonly faddy. It was simply the strangeness, simply that instead of lying flat on the plate like the meat I had been used to, the heart seemed to sit up and beg to be spared (a plea readily granted), while at the same time emitting a strong animal smell which made me decide that I was not in the least bit hungry after all. (Need I say this was years before we all learnt to queue and fight for offal of any sort?)

But it was then that I did the unforgiveable thing. I not only left the lonely heart cooling in its gravy. I tucked under the plate a note, or rather a list of culinary likes and aversions, the latter bluntly headed HEARTS, and leaving this highly inflammable tableau behind me, withdrew to an upper room.

Now, most countrywomen regard a note as most townswomen a bull: with concern and distrust. The effect of mine on old Mrs. Frost was instantaneous. No sooner had she read it than the list embarked on a shaky passage to the manor, to, in fact, my new employer, a man I particularly wanted to impress with my rural *savoir-faire*; and after the list, at arm's length, followed the incensed farmer's wife who, hobbling along with a stick, waved the paper ahead in the other trembling hand, the word "Disgusting!" popping at frequent intervals towards it, like a donkey after a dangled carrot.

For me, as parlour-boarder at Frost's, it was the end. Mrs. F. had "obliged," but I had bitten the hand that fed me or rather, rejected what it had so painstakingly prepared. In a word, my behaviour had proved "disgusting" and I must go.

Yet, as I was later to learn, there was no kinder woman in that friendly parish than my weatherbeaten, overworked old landlady. True, it was not altogether with regret that I left her lace-curtained parlour with its Haworth Parsonage view of gravestones, but the farmyard had been lively and cheerful, and by passing through it one reached Frost's mushroom fields sloping down to the very gates of a large wood, through which one could saunter to the river Evenlode.

In my first attempt at turning countryman, then, I had failed with ignominy, and now it was imperative that some other lodging should be found, and at once. One tends to think of this room-hunting as a post-war evil, and yet in the part of Oxfordshire where I was working some twelve years ago it seemed just as difficult to get a roof over one's head as it is now.

I tried cottage after cottage. Either my disgusting reputation had run before me or else there really was no spare room; or, more likely, the wives and mothers had already too many meals to see to and beds to make. In growing desperation I went on searching one evening until after ten, when I found myself at the door of the loneliest looking inn I had ever seen. There was no sign of life at all, neither light nor sound. I knocked.

At once there was uproar as from a kennel of mad dogs and then silence. I knocked again, and between bursts of barking heard rhythmic slow thumps as of an elderly someone reluctantly negotiating a long stone passage. Then bolts and chains were laboriously dealt with, and slowly, grudgingly it seemed, the door was edged open enough for Mrs. Ragley to see who it was. She saw a worried-looking young man in a town suit and heard him beg for a room. I saw a stranger with eyes full of suspicion, and held my breath for her refusal.

She stomped away with my petition, however, "to sleep on it," and next day, without even a glance at the two rooms she offered me, I took them and moved in. One of them, the bedroom, had a view. Standing on a rabbit-skin rug I looked across the road to the may tree in the low hedge and the cornfield beyond, with a little black firwood to one side of it and the weathercock on Wychwood spire seeming about to feed on the ripening wheat. I didn't know then that that may tree was the favourite singing-post of a mistle-thrush (it sang of a morning, "If you don't get *out* of bed *I* think you'll be la-a-a-ate," drawling its "a" in true Cotswold fashion), nor that the fir wood meant home to quite a colony of goldcrests; but the view as it was, with the words beyond, was more than enough. I flung the sash window wide and blessed my luck.

Downstairs was inclined to be gloomy, and since the black spaniel was chained to the foot of those stairs and you never knew which of them he had chosen to sleep under, it was as well to be careful. My sitting-room or parlour, however, with its pleasant bay window, was comparatively lively, being overlooked from the road by those sufficiently keen-eyed to penetrate Mrs. Ragley's net curtains, and from within, by the majestic subject of "Absence Makes the Heart Grow Fonder" by Marcus Stone.

It was not a picture anyone under seventy — and few over — would choose to live with to-day, and at first, glancing at the girl as she drooped against her carved beech tree, I felt nervous. There was, as Walt Whitman said (though in a somewhat different context), that lot of her and all so luscious. However, as time went on, I found myself developing for Absence a kind of sympathetic tolerance. I could not love her, she was so uncompromisingly of one's grandfather's day, but there was undoubtedly something about her. In short, I grew quite fond of her and came to feel that there was room in the Drover's Arms for us both.

My evenings were spent in a sweating endeavour to learn shorthand, but my landlady was not one to encourage the burning of midnight oil. Sharp at ten there would come her slow tread along the black passage, then the swish along the wall of her hand and the grope-rattle-turn of my door handle before her *nid-de-moineau* coiffure finally appeared . . .

"We're very *hi*-ser-lated here," she would say; to which I would nervously agree. Pause while she gazed fixedly at the lamp, and then, "You'll put the lamp out afore you go hup?" "Yes, Mrs. Ragley." "Well, we're lockin' hup now. Good night, Mr. Green." "Good night, Mrs. Ragley."

If, sickening of shorthand, I spent an evening out, I would find everything locked, bolted and barred when, at a quite ordinary hour, I returned. At such times there were two alternatives: either in darkness to find the back door key in the coal-shed, remember that the lock was upside down and that there was a black dog under one of the stairs; or to swarm up the front of the inn by way of the taproom window and the leads above it, and so into my bedroom without even smelling the spaniel, or, indeed, any of the smells otherwise encountered *en route*. Almost always I chose the window way, even though it meant a wigging from my scandalised landlady.

As for food, the sheep's heart which had led to my eviction from Frost's farm had at least taught me never to murmur about any dish set before me at the inn. No one will now believe that for the first two months I lived at the Drover's I had no meat except rabbit and no sweet except chocolate blancmange and (once) a dumpling which my landlady warned me (or at least I took it so) contained "no hordinary happle." Perhaps memory does tend to exaggerate. I remember trying to burn half an underdone pudding rather than leave it on my plate, but Mrs. Ragley never tried to tempt me with a heart, nor even a kidney. There were times when I wished she would.

In those lean days I was always popping into Mrs. Lee's little shop down in Wychwood for various kinds of chocolate (there were then at least a dozen) to help fill the gaps. It was a way of keeping alive, but my digestion revolted. Nor did things begin to look up till I became on sufficiently good terms with J, then living in a Wychwood shepherd's cottage and working with me on a country magazine, to cash in on her infinitely superior plan, which was simply to pack into a carpenter's straw hold-all everything one could legitimately lay hands on and cook it at an outdoor "camp."

Into the pan, then, went eggs, tomatoes, bacon, chippolata, potatoes, mushrooms; and these we ate with raw apple, chased down with strong Indian tea. At other times, when we were really hungry, there would be a column of crumpets oozing Frost's butter at every pore and begging to be eaten red hot with fresh watercress. Water came from a spring which ran into a large stone trough in a nearby bank and we boiled it in a billycan hung over the fire on the pothook J had been given by an old neighbour of Mrs. Frost's, one Emma Bramley.

Almost our only visitor, at that quarry-camp in the fir wood, was our young friend Peter, a large, quiet person whose way with crumpets was pretty to watch. With him would come running, on soundless pads, a pied sheepdog, and between them plates and pan would get such a scraping and licking as practically to obviate any serious washing up.

All, in fact, went idyllically until Mrs. Lee of the village shop, always first with the news, told us that "our" little wood was about to change hands and that permission to camp in its ex-quarry would most likely be withdrawn.

This meant that we had to prospect further afield and after much searching we found, just below a group of barns and horse-chestnuts known as the Warren, a

35

disused well-house let into a high grassy bank beside a wood.

The "house" was a horseshoe of well-laid dry walling, some eight feet high and six across, roofless but sheltered, and standing back from what had once been a salt way and was now a grassy track running into the wood. The well itself had long since been filled in and packed solidly with rubble, some of which, after we had cleared out the nettles and elder, I removed so that we might have instead a level floor made of the largest flat stones I could find.

For seats the old rickyard above supplied us with five mushroom-shaped staddle-stones (though we seldom entertained on that scale), a sixth, reversed, serving as fireside table and a good, firm, handy one it made. The fireplace we built at the back, at the head of the horseshoe, with an iron bar stuck in the wall to take the billycan. We still needed a cupboard, and so, in a hidden place beneath a hawthorn, I scooped one out of the bank and lined it with thin slabs of stone, a tougher job than it sounds.

J was equally energetic with her natural garden, discouraging the more pernicious weeds and making room for less pushful favourites, so that sweetbriar and toadflax spread and prospered, as did campion, mallow and the pimpernels (scarlet and the rare blue), while the violet stars and harlequin berries of woody nightshade trailed down the grey wall from the flourishing garden above.

Then there was wood and luckily plenty of it. The fir wood beside us enclosed a strange grove of dead beeches and these, with dry twigs from the spruce, kept our wood-pile well supplied with shoulder-pieces, kindling and small logs.

There was only one serious want, and that was water. There was the black-looking watercress bed and there was a stone trough filled with water of a sort, but we were not prepared to trust either. To the trough especially there clung such a sinister reputation, we felt bound to bring with us every drop of water we meant to use.

Some fifty years ago, we were told, this same trough had served a group of cottages and stables, the ruins of which remained. We still enjoyed nuts from those cottagers' hazels and mint from their tangled gardens, which at high summer would unexpectedly burst into flower with that shaggy, shockheaded herb, beloved of sick horses, called elecampane.

So far so good, but rumour went on to tell of a pestilence, probably typhoid, which had flung itself upon the poor wretches with such virulence that those few who were not carried away up and across the fields in coffins, had fled the place as though it were damned.

Some, no doubt, hearing the tale would have shunned the spot for ever, but neither of us ever sensed there the spirit of tragedy, nor saw anything more ghostlike than the lone white owl which lived among the beams in the great barn and occasionally drifted out and sailed silently over our heads. There seemed, in fact, about the whole place, barns, ruins and all, a feeling of clear happiness which sent one's load of petty worries rolling away like Christian's burden. But perhaps we were prejudiced.

37

I would not care to revisit the well-house to-day. Nettles and elder will be looking after it well enough. I much prefer to keep in my mind's eye the picture that springs to it whenever such places as railway waiting-rooms turn my thoughts that way . . . It is dark and so that the smoke shall have our favourite fragrance I have gone down beside the watercress bed to cut green willow for the fire. Looking back up the slope to the well-house I see the blaze of the fire, and J in blue jeans, prodding something — potato? — in the sizzling pan. Then suddenly a sheepdog flashes into the firelight and stands a second uncertain, tail down, glancing first at the fire and then, as though for reassurance, behind him. The dog is Peter's forerunner, and sure enough in a moment an immensely tall, broad figure blocks the light. As I cut the last willow wand there comes J's call that the meal is ready, and as I walk towards our hearth I see glow-worms, beyond the fire's radiance, shining among the grasses and harebells of the bank.

(II) EMMA BRAMLEY AND THE BRONTËS

MONDAY MORNING ON THE COMMON
BY JOYCE M. WESTRUP
Perilous trousers, hung from pegs,
wave agile unrestricted legs,
whose flowing curves, replete and free,
betoken a humanity
that rolls from bliss to super bliss
in some far rounder world than this.

An apron not to be effaced
flaunts stout if unsubstantial waist.

The sheets forswear the sober bed
whereon we nightly sleep like lead,
and in a strenuous delight
would have us bounce and bounce all night;
while pillow cases almost burst
to beg us gambol with them first.

Abandoned dusters wildly ask
when next at our appointed task,
we should not gravely dust the room,
but dance and sing and wave the broom,
and whirl about our decent heads
their flapping blues and flying reds.

In swift accord the ballet flows,
for liberated matter knows
the spirit of a singing bird.
The dish cloth's unaccustomed wings
beat to the tune the bedspread sings
in notes of red and green and white.
The clothes-props quiver with delight
that this is Monday morning, this
delirious, distended bliss.

Now let the mangle do its worst;
let bodies be austere and curst;
let linen presses hold their sway;
Here's to another washing day!

There is a hymn that reminds one that toil is to be reckoned in days, whereas of ease one must not be so unreasonable as to expect more than hours. The hours we spent up at the Warren, even when it snowed and we had to improvise a roof with a groundsheet, were decidedly happy ones. We were at that self-contained stage when it was just as well that, off-duty at least, people should not be bothered with us; and when we lit the fire in the well-house and set to work cooking and sawing we made a world that was of no trouble to anyone and yet of deep satisfaction to ourselves.

In our jobs, our days of toil, we were both working at pressure, and every morning when I heard the warning mistle-thrush and swung my feet out of the feather-bed and on to the rabbit-skin rug I wondered how on earth I was going to convince my employer that I was as efficient as any of that bunch of howling totties (as someone had rudely called his staff) already installed. Neither he nor I had seen much evidence of it as yet, but with Richard Jefferies I believed wholeheartedly in miracles, and who knew, perhaps one would happen for me that very day.

Certainly our office was unusual; but although the notion of working in a Cotswold manor house was inviting enough, there seemed always something to make me late to work — mushrooms, for instance, or turning up a cast ewe — whether I took the high Roman road with its wide verges or the lower road, in the "burrer" (shelter) in the hope of overtaking J.

As it happened, she too found the walk to the office something of an obstacle race, and on the morning I think of, a fine, misty one, making clouds of one's breath, I overtook her pulling like a steam-engine, having only just turned the steep corner out of the village and being now intent on trying to make her legs walk three times faster than they wanted to go. Why not, I asked, have set out in better time?

Always, she told me, she set out in good time, in very good time, but old Mrs. Chick lay in wait at the top of the lane ("Come and see my Granny's bonnets!" she would call, with a jerk of the thumb towards her magnificent columbines); the roadman had stopped her to insist that the fine day would prove a weather-breeder; and the village itself was pitfalls from end to end. Hound puppies had tried to eat her skirt; Judy-you-dare (a bounding mongrel) had done her best to smirch it; and Miss Skein, the seamstress (her garden gay with woodruff, which she called Lady's Needlework), had leaned out of her window to know if Miss Westrup really meant red flannel. "Yes," J had called, hurrying on, "it's not for me, you know, though it well might be."

So we hurried along together towards the manor and waved to old Emma Bramley as we passed. True gardener that she was, there was always something blooming in her garden. Even when snow lay inches deep you had only to lift an old washtub to find a nest of wide-open Christmas roses; and in the drab days of March when, except for primrose or crocus, the only scrap of colour her garden boasted was a fine scarlet petticoat on the line, the stout old gardener herself, wrinkled but rosy and bright-eyed as she sat in the

41

green shade of her "gerangers," would maintain that her garden at that very moment was "all knotted for bloom."

We found her good to listen to, her language seeming to come straight from *Cold Comfort Farm* (or maybe some of that uproarious classic came straight from her). She called an accident "the upster," asked us to excuse her "dirty dishabill," condemned a neighbour "giddy as a goose and hot as a fire coal," and told us time and time again, in words of her own minting, of the days when she washed a score of surplices for "the Reverend Moon." A laundress by day, at night there had of course been midwifery (day babies had, I suppose, to take their chance), and to hear her reminisce of death was like listening to Mistress Quickly, or of babes, to Juliet's nurse. "I'm dying," said one, and "Oh, I hope not," said she. "But I knew by her nose," she told us, "and the turn of her head, poor dear."

But it would never do for us to linger at Emma's on our way to the office. Once enclosed in that fragrarium of liniment and soapsuds and potted plants we would be there for a session and must hear of the Reverend Moon all over again. Besides, we were in no mood that morning for airy gossip, having failed the previous evening, in the shepherd's cottage at Wychwood where J lodged, to hit on the new notion we sought for the strictly commercial purpose of melting advertising agents' hearts. In pursuit of a telling tag we had more than skimmed all the Psalms, both Alices and Virgil, but without success, even though we had been buoyed up with mugs of Ovaltine and glasses of mangold-wurzel wine. For J there was the solace of an acceptance (the poem reprinted on page 38), but her official reference on the magazine was, like mine, advertising, of which she noted, "This is not my kind of work at all, but will do it once." Activity outside the office was much more to her liking, whether it was play reading or camping or seeing to the church flowers or just going the round of the village — "in and out of cottages and talking to farmers," as the editor wrote hopefully of his staff.

Only those who have tried it know how much courage, charm, persistence, patience, tact and downright hard work is needed to coax village friends to take a part and read of a winter's evening in the village hall and in front of their neighbours.

Yet to choose the play and round up a hesitant cast was but the beginning. The audience, too, expected nurture. Such was Emma Bramley's zest for all village goings-on, she insisted on attending all our play readings, though they cannot always have been to her taste. This meant that at least half an hour before the curtain J, with all a producer's worries on her mind, had to help dress her, and that was no light task. Boots, I understand, were the biggest trouble; but once they were laced the dresser turned with a lighter heart to the layers of coats and cloaks and the black hat trimmed with cock's feathers. At long last she would be ready, all except for her storm lantern, and with that swinging from one gloved hand, the other on the arm of her escort, she unhurriedly navigated the few hundred yards to the schoolhouse where, with something between a relieved sigh and a brave sufferer's groan she sank on to an inadequate, rush-bottomed chair in the middle of the front row.

During the performance itself the producer was by no means inactive. She read aloud, where necessary, the stage directions, prompted the forgetful and the fainthearted and might even lean across to delete an expletive which, on second thoughts, she feared the audience might not stomach. In Shaftesbury Avenue, of course, a snapped "My God!" distresses no one, but we were in the Cotswolds and in Cotswold drawl the blasphemy of "My Go-o-o-o-od!" was appalling.

What Emma Bramley made of John Sangster's *The Brontës* we shall never know. Garrulous on many subjects, she seldom committed herself either in praise or blame on our more or less ambitious dramatic offerings. But somehow I think she enjoyed our bearded editor as Brontë senior — a fearsomely dignified interpretation — especially when in the last act he found himself faced with his profligate son, whom he thought he had buried, reincarnated in the somewhat tediously innocuous form of his son-in-law — the Reverend Arthur Bell Nicholls! The play went well to a packed house, and for myself, in spite of having to double those two opposite parts, I never enjoyed an evening more, my one regret being that my father (so wholehearted an admirer of the sisters as to make Brontë my middle name) could not witness this rather curious repetition of a play he had applauded with enthusiasm on its first night.

The next day happening to be Mrs. Bramley's birthday, we took her a small trough with growing crocuses. The trough was the most prized in J's collection. She had several from the young mason "up the strit," the same whose stone owls (quite good ones) perched upon his dry-stone wall (still better) advertised his skill. But this one was an antique and had, so they said, served its day as rot-proof foundation for a gate-post, its special charm for the present owner lying in the light green patina that now covered it, suggestive of bright moss . . . But how foolish to forget that our old friend was something more than gardener and flower-lover, that she was in fact first and foremost a meticulous washerwoman! The trough, when its flowers had withered, was returned as clean and fresh as a Tuesday morning pinafore. You could almost smell the starch.

When we first knew the old woman her washing days, as a professional, were almost over. She did still "oblige" at one of the big houses; but then came the day when, arrived in the huge old-fashioned kitchen (built to the same scale as herself) she found that "her" ironing had been done by another and that the job allotted her that afternoon was not washerwoman's work at all, but something involving the picking over of feathers. At this the specialist's pride welled up in her till she exploded and with "Them as does the ironin' can do the feathers!" — and of course a toss of the cock's-feather hat — she walked out, never to return.

The cottage she lived in — a new, semi-detached nonentity run up by a benevolent council — she hated.

She was for ever wishing herself back in the old thatched place which had been "modernized" for somebody else; though while she had lived in it she had called it her "hovel." Obviously there was no modernizing *her*. At eighty plus, she was about as modern as Mrs. Tiggy-Winkle and just as unlikely to take kindly to transplanting. Indeed, she was just that same comfortable shape. You had only to look at her to realize that she never would "go" with a house and garden, however hygienic, that had nothing round to them but only uncompromising right-angles and sharp edges. Of course, there were nice big breezy windows which she kept closed, and she shut out the glare with a score or so of potted geraniums (it would never do to be without privacy and a screen through which to peep at passers-by). She even managed to introduce her old familiar smells of liniment and soapsuds and so oust the strange new ones the builders had left behind; but still it wasn't the same. As for health, her type takes some killing, whether it forgets its rheumatics among the bean rows or broods over them in a prefabricated hut.

I forget which of the old-lady illnesses it was that carried her off to a hospital in the East End of London, near the home of her daughter. It was, of course, even less "like" her, that ether-smelling infirmary, than her council cottage had been, and the primroses one took only seemed to give added point to the cold briskness and unhomeliness of the place. She bore it all well enough (she had met pain before and, full of grumbles over small "upsters" though she often was, knew how to face it), for all that one could see her thinking "This is none of I." I used to feel desolate about her. All I could think of for cheerfulness was the raking over of little Cotswold happenings — people, flowers, yes, even play-readings and church bazaars — and at the same time I tried to raise my own spirits with the thought that, worn and wrinkled as she was, she was in those last spring days all knotted for bloom.

When she died, as she soon did, she left us her toasting-fork, which we still use, a tough old cloak and her best saucepans. She left also the iron pothook I have mentioned, a stout affair on which her mother had hung and boiled the family kettle when they all went gleaning seventy years and more ago. It was left "for Miss Westrup," as J then was, "to go gypsying with," and in the view of at least one amateur gypsy no pothook was ever put to better use.

(III) LOWER FARM

As time went on, although far from sated with gypsying we realized that sooner or later we should have to find a house with something more substantial for roof than a groundsheet; and so in a rather desultory way we began looking about us. We soon found that in the Cotswold villages we favoured, everyone had lived in his cottage since creation, or so it appeared, and meant to go on living there till the last trump, possibly longer. Which of course was as it should be. For strangers (J had lived in the district only nine years), vacant possession seemed out of the question, and indeed it was only by chance — and curiosity — that after months of increasingly earnest searching our hunt ended, temporarily at least, at Lower Farm.

When you come upon a farm hand at work some miles from his village, you may — noticing these small things as you never would notice them in a town — wonder why. You may even, if you have what is politely called an enquiring nature and less politely sheer out and out inquisitiveness, risk the obvious retort and ask the reason.

This, in fact, when J saw Jack Shirley of Fardle laying a hedge beyond Wychwood, is precisely what she did. Why, she asked bluntly, was he working so far afield? Why, bless her, because he had moved from the place at Fardle months back. And who then was living in it now? No one . . . Without further questions J ran back to the village and, panting, scribbled a card on the postman's bonnet, his red van's bonnet, and addressed it to the farmer-landlord; and that was how our life at Fardle — a big farmstead with fields running up to the wood which stretches to the Evenlode — began.

Lower Farm was a low grey house, a hundred yards from the road and looking south on to a rising grass meadow called Cowpen. It was old enough for no one to know anything of its beginnings and so inconspicuous that though nothing but a barn and its own waggonshed stood between it and our regular route to the river, I had never even seen it until I found myself paying its modest rent.

When I did take a good look at it, inside and out, I was at first disappointed. The stone roof and walls were sound and beautiful, but inside, beneath rubble and cobwebs and peeling paper the good bones of the house were so well hidden, it needed faith as well as imagination to see what might be instead of what was.

It had been built originally as a small farmhouse of three largish rooms and three small ones, with stables added at the back to form a side of the farmyard. For a farmer of large family it would have been too small, and no doubt that was why a bigger and less attractive house (our landlord's) had later been put up on the far side of Back Orchard, Lower Farm then being converted into two labourer's cottages. At the time we took over, the dividing wall had been demolished, but we still had two staircases and two front doors, and the first thing J did was to polish their brass numbers, 16 and 17.

Number 16 had housed our friend the hedger, but 17 had been unlived-in for fifteen years, and its kitchen, with boarded windows, used as a store for implements and bicycles, while upstairs, on that side, floor and window-seats had rotted through. Altogether it seemed best to write off 17 as beyond repair.

It so happened that while the house was being taken over I had to be in London, but I remembered the advice of a father with whom moving from road to road in a suburb had been an ardently practised hobby, and putting first things first, I wired: "SEE ABOUT DRAINS AND MAKE AN AGREEMENT."

J, equally innocent, thought it best to comply. Old Steer, like most farmers, was not easy to corner, and, being deaf, still less easy to address. At last, however, she lured him to our gate, and, applying cupped hands to his ear, yelled "DRAINS?" For a moment he seemed stupefied. He stood quite still and with his small eyes looked at her as though she had struck him. Then a light dawned and without a word he led her to a large Cotswold stone trough which, seemingly for some hundreds of years, had stood against the south wall of our mediaeval house. Above this trough and brushed by a cabbage rose there was a tap — a good-natured tap, as it turned out, for it never froze — and it was to the jumble of stones underneath this trough, where the water ran gurgling away, that the fat farmer now pointed.

We were to find later that this "drain" was the home not only of a rat but of a large grass-snake (they worked a Box & Cox system), but that of course was not what Steer had meant to imply. This, he silently intimated, was the only drain at Lower Farm that he knew of; and as for an agreement, he would sign nothing, but "agreed" to let us stay till he sold the farm, "if we didn't quarrel."

As things turned out, we stayed three years and never did openly quarrel with our landlord; though as every such tenant knows, one is perpetually at the farmer's mercy, whether it's horses kicking all night against your wall or cows churning your "drive" into mire or calves among your vegetables or something worse, all of which you are expected, in the sacred name of Agricultural Priority, to bear uncomplainingly and laugh off as best you may.

It was only when our tenancy there was drawing to a close that we learnt how lucky we had been to have been "accepted" at all. Our home, our future, our very reputation, all, as it transpired, had hung on three words from the local blacksmith. "He asked what sort of folk you were," the smith, in an unusually expansive moment, told us, "and I said, 'They're all right.'" And on that verdict alone we had been accorded the entrée to Lower Farm.

Of course, no sooner had "Miss Westrup's tack," as J's few things were referred to, been brought down on a waggon from Wychwood and my own sticks added, than we realized that we should after all most certainly need the almost derelict half of the house, the half we knew as Number 17. Workmen of various grades of skill were already with us, and we now added to their number Wychwood's great carpenter, the husband of its characterful shopkeeper, Lee himself

What with builders stirring their cement puddings in the kitchen, and the Cotswolds' best polisher and their second-best (her young mistress) furiously at work on the elm boards, the little house began to be rather full; so full, in fact, that after Lee had managed to spend a day carpentering on his own, we found nailed to one of the beams a blunt note in thick carpenter's-pencil. It ran —

LESS WOMEN MORE WORK

just that.

But when at last all was done, we set our only chair, a rocker, beside the fire, put yarrow in a green glass jug on a bookcase and then sat on the window-seat of our cream-papered parlour to admire it. There was nothing

51

pseudo about the old flagged room, its proportions were fine. Must we clutter it, we wondered, with rugs and pictures and chairs? The only picture we wanted — Caracci's *Man Eating Beans* — couldn't be bought. The stone floor had to have matting, but for furniture we would have only essentials: a kitchen table, some plain chairs, shelves, and for these J bid at sales and scoured the junk shops. "Looked at furniture till worn out," runs a note typical of that time, "spent threepence." We indulged in no ornaments but had luck with such odds and ends as an old wooden flourbin (a shilling) and copper scales a hundred years old, which, with their original dated brass weights, cost us ten shillings.

Upstairs, the bedroom that was going to be ours was bare indeed. J was camping there on a folding bed for the time being, while I decorously slept at Wychwood, but apart from considerations of comfort, the room itself, with its polished boards and its green view of Cowpen, deserved, or so we thought, a princely four-poster of a kind seldom found outside museums, and when found, quite beyond the means of about-to-be-weds who had doubts about the extravagance of taking on a small farmhouse at a rent of ten shillings a week.

When I first saw it in the upstairs lumber-room of an antique shop in Burford I thought, "A beauty, but not for us." True, it had no canopy, but it had everything else: carving — good carving — on the headboard, and at the foot two polished wooden bosses each the size of a boy's head. It was of oak and a good colour, but it looked too short. Indeed, it only needed my six foot

52

and a bit laid beside it on the floor of the shop to prove the deficiency and decide me against it . . . J then declared that she must have it. It was taken to pieces. It was lengthened. It was conveyed six miles and with curses coaxed up our winding stair. It was reassembled, and all — yes, including the cost of the bed itself — for £12 10s. Then, seeing it stand there so sturdily, oak on elm, you would have said that it was the only bed for that room, that it had been made for it. Even the fleurs-de-lis in the headboard might have known the same hand as had shaped our mullions; and the quilt of candlewick cotton, like distant plough-land with the sun on it, gave the finishing touch.

It was just as we had all we wanted how we wanted it, even to the bowl Peter had turned for us and the feather-pattern curtains he had designed and dyed, that we were invaded by family furniture: magnificent oak dresser, tables, a small bed — and the Brontë Chair, a chair sat on by the sisters when they went visiting Top Withen (Wuthering Heights), and bought at Sotheby's by my father, to whose admiration for the sisters I have already referred. All this assortment of old furniture went in, and the house, which may well have seen similar stuff before, accepted it with good grace; but we still thought that we had liked it better bare.

Out of doors there was all too obviously plenty for amateurs to do. Against the east wall of the house, for instance, where it made a corner with the wood-shed, there was a dump of solid rubbish which must have been accumulating for years. It was no use feeling fastidious or pausing to speculate on the mentality of those who foul their own nest. When the time came to tackle it the combined onslaught was so concentrated that the unsavoury jetsam — old tins, old batteries, old stays and worse — was hustled out of sight and disposed of in scarcely more time than it took to gasp disgust. In its place we grew a grass plot where, in days to come, breakfasts of grapefruit, coffee, toast, Mrs. Frost's butter and Mr. Cooper's unexpurgated marmalade (all heaven sent) were savoured and appreciated to the full.

The garden as we found it had a damson and several plum trees including, on the south wall, a Magnum Bonum which gave us the finest yellow plums I have tasted.

As for flowers and vegetables, J had to rise earlier and earlier to keep pace with generosity. "Given phlox and mimulus," she noted, "Given raspberry canes and shallots and pink chrysanthemums," "Given a blue primrose plant by Mrs. Chick," "Car full of plants from Abbotswood," and so on, till it was difficult to find half a square foot of soil for a latecomer.

The herb garden, too, began to take shape, charmingly irregular shape with plumes of feathery fennel, a cushion of thyme, a bush of old man, a clump of red bergamot, a border of parsley, a snippet of this and a sliver of that: rue, lavender, liquorice, sage, marjoram, rosemary, tarragon, mint, basil — "simples of a thousand names," and all growing within two steps of the kitchen door.

54

When the great day came our guests exclaimed at the show of phloxes and tiger lilies, scabious, larkspur, hellenium, mallow and the rest. How delightfully natural, they said, these cottage gardens were, they just grew themselves. Only the handful of gardeners among them guessed what it had cost to get that brick path weeded and scrubbed and thrift-bordered, and that burgeoning heliotrope in its pocket-handkerchief bed looking as though it had just occurred.

Most of the guests were concerned at the shortcomings indoors: no bathroom, no water-closet not even a sink, and nothing better to cook by or sit by than an old blackleaded range! No bathroom meant a washtub by the fire and on warm days a scrub down in the big stone trough outside. No indoor lavatory meant, among other things, a blow of fresh air whatever the weather. In summer it had the attractions of a gardener's bothy, our lilac-shaded privy, and it made a capital place for musing on the garden's crops; nor, with its view of bird-box and the birds that foraged among the bean-sticks (including a lesser-spotted woodpecker), was it to be scorned as an ornithologist's hide. There was also the wren that nested behind the door.

There were drawbacks, of course. The privy might get snowed up entirely overnight, or a passing soldier in the weighty accoutrements of battle ("readin' and smokin' and makin' a weddin' of it," as a commiserator guessed) might, and in fact did, break the seat clean in two; but neither mishap was irremediable, and although I did the spadework myself I decided, at least when the

55

damson was in bloom and the mistle-thrush singing in the orchard, that I wouldn't change places with anyone, no not with the most sumptuously porcelained and mahoganied millionaire.

As for the old oven, one seldom heard anything but praise of it from the cook who, though inexperienced, coaxed it to send sizzling to table, times without number, such meals as draw the heart out in thanksgiving and leave the stomach replete but light.

Every house has its smell — lavender, tobacco, boarding-house stew. Lower Farm smelt of beeswax and sometimes of chicken or chopped parsley or fervently cherished leek-and-potato soup. There would probably be a smell of wood-smoke too, for the fire liked willow or thorn, oak, apple, ash, or even elm, provided it was seasoned, along with the coal. It was the fire indeed that was the living heart of the house, the living-room fire that heated both room and oven. One slaved for it in all weathers and on days when it was not in the vein cursed it for the dead-alive thing it chose to be. But to step into the room at the end of a day's walking and know its welcome (for in those carefree days it was left well banked), to set it to brown potato cakes on a girdle (was it fourteen Peter ate?), and to sit at dusk and watch the firelight on oak and brass and pewter, and on features too . . . yes, those were times when blessings needed no counting, nor was the old black-leaded grate, with its cage of flames, by any means the least of them.

As we sat by it our feet rested on a rag rug with a bold star worked in its middle. It had been a wedding present from old Mrs. Chick, a neighbour of J's at Wychwood, the same that had given her a blue primrose plant. Some of the rags had, in their pride and hers, played their part in the daily upholstering of Emma Bramley, while the star of hope itself was of hunting pink discarded by no less a personage than a local peer. It was a magnificent rug, deep and tough and handsome and had, as we well knew, taken the old woman months to make. Indeed, we had questioned her about it, as she sat amid countless framed photographs of babies, and had received a short answer. It was a Special Order, we were told; and that was all. As our wedding day approached, however, and the star took on its full brilliance, she admitted that the rug was for us and that she had been praying for our happiness as she made it.

(IV) COTSWOLD PATCHWORK

At the time when we were settling into Lower Farm I had not even heard of the late local celebrity Warde Fowler, humanist and naturalist, who had written so wisely and well about this very district, and in particular about its birds and flowers.

The fact is, his books — "A Year with the Birds," "Summer Studies" and the rest — are not nearly so well known as they deserve, though those of us who have them are inclined to speak of them so well that our copies are constantly on loan to the uninitiated; so much so, indeed, that I sometimes think it cannot be long before the delightful old don is rediscovered and made much of and accorded the niche that must assuredly await him not so very far from Gilbert White's.

It has been said of Warde Fowler by a fellow traveller that whenever there was anything of interest to be seen he always managed to be looking out of the carriage window. And even less likely was the possibility of his missing anything noteworthy as he walked his favourite footpaths, whether they led him beside the Evenlode, with its yellow water-lilies, forget-me-nots, codlins-and-cream and flowering rush, or across it and through "our" wood to the switchback meadows and the high ridge beyond, where, having climbed at a good pace with his friend the Captain, he would call for drinks at the Drover's Arms.

Dipping into his writings now I come across references to uncommon-plant localities the secret of which we had thought of as peculiarly ours, and I feel a glow for the man — "the sort," as he writes of another, "whom every honest dog would love" — as he nimbly touches upon them without giving one direct clue as to precise whereabouts.

"The bright blue cornflower (*Centaurea cyanus*)," he notes, "is local, and there is only one field known to me where it grows abundantly, and in the society of the yellow chrysanthemum, making a never-to-be-forgotten glory of colour in July and August." Never-to-be-forgotten indeed! Every summer we made a point of walking over to see it.

He found as we did, once only, the blue pimpernel, and considered the large blue cranesbill (*Geranium pratense*) "the most beautiful of all our flowers." (To us

58

it has always seemed *the* flower of the Cotswolds, at its best along the verges of a rough old lane like that which overlooks the Windrush between Burford and Little Barrington.) Of our greatest botanical find in that neighbourhood, however, he says nothing, and since, shrewd old bird that he was, he is most unlikely to have overlooked it, I shall certainly not presume to be more confiding. Suffice it to say, then, that the flower was a wood flower of great beauty, shown us on oath by a farm labourer, and that when we heard of its discovery by a local bigwig (a power-behind-the-Government, who had lately settled at Wychwood), we trembled for the little patch. The great man, however, contented himself with cuttings, thereby sending his stock rocketing in our esteem and leaving the flower-clump to go on blooming and spreading in a most enheartening way.

Rarity-hunting for its own sake is a specialist's hobby, abounding (with luck in thrills, but for quiet day to day enjoyment there are in almost any wood lesser surprises, lesser that is in rarity, though not by any means in beauty. I remember well in our wood the veined white flowers and shamrock leaves of a certain wood-sorrel cluster rooted among moss on a rotten oak stump some four feet from the ground, the intrinsic beauty of flower and leaf intensified by nearness and by the strangeness of their position, which normally, of course, would be close to the ground. The delicacy of the flowers (the same Miss Mitford raved over), the freshness of the leaves and the neat compactness of the whole casual "arrangement" were altogether delightful, so that the bramble patch beside which they grew became for us a place to be visited often, not only for its white admirals and fritillaries, but also for the common wood-sorrel which year after year "corsaged" that dead tree.

We spent much time in the wood. It was so old, so large and secluded, so richly stocked — I never saw honeysuckle cascade as it did here from the very tops of oak trees — and withal so peaceful and so kind there seemed often no point in going farther afield. It was the sort of wood of which Anatole France must have been thinking when he wrote, "Les bois surtout sont tendres à l'homme. Dieu en a fait des asiles sacrés où la paix s'habite et l'harmonie du monde se révèle." We would take food and, leaving it in the wood hut, wander off perhaps to the most secluded glade of all, the one with the great tree in it which we knew as Henry's Beech.

From the carvings on the trunk it was obvious that this hidden dell had once been a favourite trysting-place. But the carved hearts and arrows were almost all faint and fading, as though the way to the tree were no longer generally known or lovers too stay-at-home or cinema-loving or even fainthearted. Only one addition looked at all recent: the initials of our farmer-landlord's son Henry, which stood out boldly enough and in sharp contrast to those of his great-grandfather, whose pierced heart now shone but dimly from a point a little higher up the trunk.

If lovers still courted there they were too sophisticated to leave initials. We met no one, and indeed in all that great wood and at all times the chances of meeting another soul were small. One might possibly happen on a cheerful family of freckled children (of whom I hope to say more) or a horseman in a fury at having lost the hunt, but no one else; so that when there had been a snowfall almost all the tracks were of bird and wild animal, with only once, as I remember, the large prints of a man's boots, which we knew to be Peter's, leading as it were enquiringly to the wood hut and back again, with the light pad marks of a sheepdog close beside them.

"They fear not men in the woods," wrote Kipling, "because they see so few," words which came to mind often in those bosky days when, walking softly, we might disturb an old ginger fox taking his ease on a bed of flattened bluebells or surprise a tangle of grass-snakes sunning themselves on fallen leaves. I say "surprised," but I wonder, were fox and snakes as surprised as we were? Are they not, even when half asleep in the safest-seeming place, perpetually on the qui vive? For my part (and no doubt the experience is general), to be surprised by wild creatures at close quarters is to see them with such intensity that each separate hair, scale — or, more commonly, feather — seems to bypass the eye and imprint itself directly and permanently upon the mind.

But then who has not suddenly seen a kingfisher and been left gasping at the almost tangible impact of that shrill, unEnglish blue streaking between the homely greens and browns of reeds and rushes "like a waif from some far tropical land"? Were the kingfisher as common and confiding as the robin, it is just conceivable that we might tire of his brightness. As it is, our enjoyment — intense, concentrated — is by the second only; and so the kingfisher remains, in Hudson's phrase, "perhaps the most medicinal of all birds to see."

Of the bolder and duller-hued birds that forced themselves on our attention at Lower Farm, none seemed more aggressive, in early spring, than a certain mistle-thrush which, perched high in an elm beside the orchard, cursed anything in fur, feather or tweed happening within sight. There are few songs, to my ear, more compelling than the sad-sweet, desultory, disillusioned, take-it-or-leave-it plaint of the mistle-thrush, but I do not care for the bird when it is out of temper, nor when it hits on a near-human inflexion, as did this one, and broadcasts the same phrase several hundred times a day. "Carefully, carefully," sang our bird, "where y' goin'?" And then almost without pause, triumphantly as it seemed, "Incidentally, you're on the rocks!" Nor was this gloomy message varied from spring to spring. It had chosen its singing-post well. Beneath it frothed the orchard with its hundred good, mossy nesting-sites, and so favoured was that orchard with sun that on the little hedge-bank enclosing it on the south, cowslip and white violet came into flower at least six clear weeks before one might hopefully look for them anywhere else.

Much of our time, then as now, was spent in wooding, and from wood and orchard we carried back such odds and ends as the trees had discarded. Thorn, oak, beech, ash, all found their way to the sawing-horse the hurdler had given us, as did fragrant apple, cherry and willow; but elm, unless well seasoned, was seldom worth the carrying; the wood of conifers, too, we left behind. Gradually the floor of the woodshed became deeply carpeted in sawdust and dead leaves intermixed with knots of oak, slivers of willow and all manner of chips and twigs and knobbly bits which to the seeker of morning's-wood or kindling mean treasure trove.

It may be that all the world over farmers' wives arrange trugs of this morning's wood with meticulous neatness — the very smallest and slimmest of twigs at one end, chopped branch the other, with perhaps a trimming of tempting oddments tucked in here and there, to be added by the experienced fire-builder at the precise place and moment — or they may get a skilled hand to chop and arrange it and stand it ready beside the fire for next day. At our farmstead at all events, morning's-wood was taken seriously, the standard being set by a little old rough-looking fellow whose filled trug stood on the worn flagged floor of our landlord's kitchen, looked as though Rumplestiltskin had been at work in a housewife's dream.

About most of these remote farmsteads, unless of course the place has been turned into one vast roaring, horseless and hedge-less factory, there hangs a deceptive sleepiness, workers and animals alike toning in with their background, heads down to hoeing or cropping or whatever it may be. It took much to rouse Fardle; to make a man look up from his muckrake or a beast from its feed. But when Henry's Circus took the field, when of a drowsy afternoon Henry, the farmer's son, came whooping across Cowpen in the fodder cart drawn by galloping Jack, his white pony, and the terrier Gyppie ran barking at the wheels, the whole farm was suddenly "on the look," while Atchie the pet lamb confidently trotted forward to meet her master.

And what, we asked Henry, was the derivation of that name Atchie? He couldn't say. For as long as he could remember and his father could remember, whenever there was a pet lamb on that farm it had been called Atchie, and here was this year's pet growing finer and woollier every day, a veritable Mouton Rothschild in whose fleece you might lose your hand. We had known her since gambolling babyhood when, under the apple trees and with all the bright young orchard-grass at her door, she had been quartered in a modest zinc hutch called The Palace Coop. As she grew older she was given the freedom of Cowpen and left to make what she could of the small dairy herd which usually lived there. From our windows she appeared aloof and mystified. For some days she would have none of them, feeding as far from them as she could and trotting to us most readily for titbits whenever we appeared. The cows, however, inquisitive as cows always are, made advances, and with wary looks and much puffing surrounded her, which Atchie, after some hesitation, took to mean acceptance as one of the herd.

Thenceforward Atchie went with the cows, so that when they were called for milking she had to be stopped at the orchard gate and turned back. She seemed, indeed, to have quite resigned herself to being one of them, when there came that misty morning which brought us, before we were up, a scurrying whisper, and looking out I saw a flock of sheep pour past the gate and into Cowpen, where immediately they began eating, their little puffs of breath adding to the surrounding mist.

Atchie's bewilderment was plain to see. She stood apart, with no attempt to feed or to join them, and ever and anon she would gaze earnestly at our windows as though for guidance or possibly to reassure her old friends that she had not the least thought of deserting them.

But as time went on and the nibbling flock enveloped her, Atchie, like a Labour peer, found herself one of them willy-nilly and gradually borne away on an irresistible tide of woolly kinship she withdrew more and more openly from those with whom she had so lately gone proudly friended. She would not look at a cow, and as for us . . . "Atchie!" we called, and at first she came, but then sensed the others all watching, and, growing self-conscious, bundled back again thankfully, her one wish to be like all the rest, an inconspicuous part of God's woolwork. It was yet another tribute to the power of public opinion and of that gregarious instinct to conform which so many people seem to inherit direct from the flock.

(V) SOME COTSWOLD NEIGHBOURS

When there were houses to be had it used to be the privilege of the townsman, if you could call it a privilege, to move house as often as he liked without exciting any out-of-the-way comment. No one that I remember from boyhood, except our family and the perspiring men who had undertaken to move us (including the six who carried my father's sundial-base: a Giant's Causeway column), took anything but the mildest interest in our almost continuous move from road to road (indistinguishable as they were) in one of Croydon's dormitory suburbs.

In the country, on the other hand, where most people would as soon think of moving as of trying to transplant a full-grown oak, such a happening could never go unremarked. When J had moved from Frost's Farm at Mulberry to the Perrys' cottage in the next village (Wychwood), a farmer whose land adjoined Frost's had taunted her with, "You bin too high now, simly, to live along o' we poor folk!" And when it came to leaving Wychwood for Fardle, Hannah Lee, who kept the shop at Wychwood, solemnly warned her (albeit with a twinkle), "You'll pine away, child."

It was true that normally the only people to come near us at Lower Farm, apart from our landlord, his son and his farmhands Dick and Harry (Harry had been born on our bedroom floor at a time when no one except himself and his mother could be spared from getting in the harvest), were the pale-eyed roadman who was always harrying the weeds where our mud-drive joined the road; and four postmen upon whom we came to rely not only for local tidings richly but for four more or less soundly-reasoned and plain-spoken outlooks on current world affairs.

On our part, to the man who took his turn of our mud and mails, and of his own good nature kept us posted as to woldly and worldly doings (we might even be shown how to improve a rose-bush with a clothes-peg or be treated to a well-weighed talk on lasting peace), to this rare caller, whose very boots seeped beauty as they released their mud on the flags at our two front doors, could we in common kindness do less than offer a cup of tea? Monstrous, indeed, it would have been to deny him, and folly too, for we would undoubtedly have been the losers.

Many then were the mugs of tea downed by postmen at Lower Farm. Many too, and sometimes very surprising were the scraps of wisdom that came to us over the steaming tops of the blue-and-white ringed mugs. True, I remember little of that wisdom now, it was frothy stuff mostly, but I shall always hear Jack, oldest and cheeriest of the four, call out, "Ah well, we can't all . . ." as, after a long talk, he swung off into the mud on the way to his van, and I shall go on vaguely wondering what exactly it was that we couldn't all of us do or have.

Anthony Trollope, you may remember, in his *Last Chronicle of Barset*, writes of a postman who went in dread of being watched. He was invited to "come in and warm theeself a while," but — "'Well,' said Robin, 'I dudna jist know how till be. The werry 'edges 'as eyes and tells on me in Silverbridge if I so much as stops to pick a blackberry.' . . . She handed him a bowl of tea and a slice of buttered toast."

A tale of long ago. And yet that, we were asked to believe, was precisely the situation with which we were faced just then at Lower Farm! There were watchers, said postie, peeping Toms (or it may have been Tabbies) who, plain to his view, lurked behind hedges and timed him; thanks, however, to his setting out early, with a liberal provision of time for a pause at Fardle, Jack could, so he averred, afford to laugh at such spies and openly did so.

To us, of course, the whole situation seemed too Gilbertian to be true. But then came the sad day when, in quadruplicate, there arrived that stern notice from Head Office. It was headed:

LOITERING AND UNNECESSARY CONVERSATION.

This impertinence our four friends were of course as one man for ignoring, but after more unnecessary conversation and coaxing and a second helping of the same notice, again in quadruplicate, they agreed (more in pity for their bosses than as an admission of the slightest dereliction on their own part) to comply.

"Bother," was the disappointed hostess's comment, "loitering and unnecessary conversation are my two favourite things . . . Tea is off."

There still remained as a potential guest the ancient roadman, a wan creature for ever busy about the verges with archaic implements propelled with frail hands and chest. At J's earnest request he had spared some particularly fine clumps of roadside bedstraw, and so surely he might be lightly rewarded with tea or even beer? But oh dear no, he dursn't neither. "They comes round s'quick," he said hoarsely, with a nervous glance over his shoulder, "there's three on 'em at it." So. Ruthless wage-slavery had penetrated even to the remotest corners of the Cotswolds. Yet who would have dreamt, watching his lonely, unhurried scrabblings, that here went yet another downtrodden hireling, haunted by overseers whizzing round hot on each other's heels to make certain that the ancient was ever doggedly at it rather than letting the grass grow under his feet? It came home to us then how wrong we had been to tempt him, even though we had never once penetrated his masters' disguise.

If then, as occasionally happened, we felt in need of company and there seemed no one about, there was but one thing to do and that was to leave Fardle and take the field way — Cowpen, Wetfoot, Yallands and the rest — to Wychwood, there to consort with old friends to whom a good gossip was as cheerful a way of redeeming the time as any they knew and so much more satisfying than the wireless, which you couldn't answer back or argue with or persuade to listen to your own little story, however superior that story might seem to you to be.

Wychwood was, in fact, as we well knew, a warmhearted little stronghold of independence, and arrived there we would make our way first to the village shop, and that not so much on account of what we might buy there — though the place was a marvel of compactness and stocked exotic kinds of chocolate never seen before or since — no, not nearly so much for that as for Hannah Lee's amiable talk which, in a remarkably short time, would bring us up to the minute with village news.

In nearly every village, just as there is one man capable and good-natured enough to turn a hand to pretty nearly anything, so there is a woman of the comfortable, experienced sort — wise, discreet, dependable to the last safety-pin — to mother that village from birth on. In an emergency she is the first her neighbours would think to send for, but somehow she is already there, in sickroom or kitchen, to be relied on as midwife, nurse, cook, clerk, general skivvy or even priest and confessor, according to need. Of such was Hannah Lee.

And was she proud of her sons! Talking idly with J, as women will, of babies, "Such a lovely little bum he had," she mused fondly, "our Cyril . . ." "And still has!" laughed an eighteen-year-old giant, who had been eavesdropping, popping his head round the door.

But Hannah was worried that day about old Mrs. Chick (the maker of rag rugs) who had "had an attack," and she (Hannah), too tied to the shop to go and see to her. It relieved her to know that Angelina Chick's was our next port of call; though when we reached the gate with hop and woodbine (as she called it) arched over it we were surprised to see the familiar small figure in black pottering as usual about her exposed garden in the detached, indifferent seclusion of the deaf. Yes, she agreed, she had been took bad, a very bad go this time, but now, thanks be, she felt better than ever, and how did we think her garden was looking?

We thought, for a woman who had produced seventeen children and yet still did all the work of her cottage and garden, pretty good. Indeed, as is usually the way with these seeming-casual old-women gardeners, every seed she wanted to grow did grow and every cutting she struck obligingly flourished. But then who knows what prayers or incantations she muttered over them? She banked on miracles (the pictures on the seed packets promised as much), and thanks to the patron saint of gardening and old countrywomen, pulling his weight with her own faith and magic and industry, she seldom was disappointed. Furthermore, although of course she never would have admitted it even to herself, I think it must have been to some minor saint or god of gardening that she reared and kept on rearing her grottoes. Possibly she built them by moonlight, for one never saw her at it. Glancing over the low wall one would suddenly become aware of a complete, new grotto — ferns, cockleshells and all — and I often wondered where that tiny old frame of hers found strength to pile up the heavy stones. From time to time the grottoes would be added to — a cushion of thrift here, a "paincher" (broken china) there — as though in thanks for protection from some specially virulent plague of slugs or snails; and one had only to glance at neighbouring gardens to see how the charm had held.

And what, J enquired, was that pretty, bright-blue flower growing at her feet? She looked down. Oh that, she chuckled. That must have sprouted from Dicky's seed — the cleanings from the birdcage!

The magic that hung over Mrs. Chick's gardening, we found, coloured her whole life. She knew, for instance, that were one to make Good Friday a washing-day (not of course that such an enormity was to be thought of), the water would turn to blood. Though what one lost through such foolhardiness might just possibly be redeemed by the right wish at the next new moon. J, seeing the slim crescent one night above the old woman's cottage, ran in and told her. Without a word she ran out in her stockinged feet, into the rough lane, and bobbed it a curtsey.

She was eighty-four when she took the field way — and a very rough way it was — to Lower Farm, and as she swept our paths with her skirts, pounced on almost invisible weeds. On her way, she told us, she had looked into the wood and the waste of good kindling she had seen was "sinful."

She must have been close on ninety when, after long absence, I returned to Wychwood on a visit. But how can "My *word!*" which was all she said for a full minute as she took both my hands, convey the warmth of her welcome? Deaf as she was, words were nothing to her. But to one at least of those who knew her even to think of her now brings a glow.

At the foot of the short rough lane that ran down past Mrs. Chick's, and, as far as one could see from the green where it started, ended in a big apple tree, there lived our friend and J's former landlord Dick Perry. His house was decidedly one to envy him for, being sturdy and full of sun which steadily brought to perfection the giant Williams hanging over the front door. Often it smelt of honey, and for some years it was wont to contain himself, his wife, his little daughter freckled like a robin's egg, and J; but there was never the least question as to who was master in it or who was wearing what Trollope calls "that garment which is supposed to denote virile command." "Steady and manful" were Dick's watchwords, never "random and prodigal" like less responsible folk.

As a shepherd with his dogs he was tremendous, shouting, commanding, full of strange oaths which only dogs — and sometimes not even dogs — understood. As a talker, pipe in hand, he was good to listen to, whether it was of a ewe he had to tell that had strayed after "sweet pickings from the water ditch" or the new boy-chap they had taken on to help him, "no more use than a capful o' crabs."

We asked him one morning to show us the lark's nest he had found down the Green Lane. Too busy to come himself he gave us detailed directions, the crux of them being, as I gathered, a certain "gret stwun" and an equally significant "pibble." When we came to that stwun we were to leave the path and take so many paces to the west till we reached the pibble, close to which we would see the nest. Sure enough we found it, just as he had said, the warm brown eggs glossy in their haycup, as one remembered them from childhood. Nor did we fail to mark the shepherd's distinction: the stone was a rough chunk of Cotswold sandstone, the pebble, smooth and rounded, must have spent an age or so under the sea.

There were times when he seemed to regard his parlour-boarder as just another obstreperous ewe and "'ooman," he would blurt out, "why doesn't thee use thy bloomin' yed?" But in more modest humour he would go so far as to seek her opinion, and "That's quite right what you say, Miss Westrup" then became a flatteringly common phrase. One evening he took a stray bee she had found and lodged it for the night in a disused kennel. . . . "And if that's man enough to seek the hive in the marnin', that's up to ee, byent it?"

There was no doubt that he enjoyed hearing his own yarns, and on occasion, before embarking on country matters — farmyard affairs, I mean, involving the idiosyncrasies of stock — he would, as it were, flourish a Certificate A by reminding J that she was "a woman in years"; while at the close of the anecdote he might ask for his audience's discretion for the dumb brutes' behaviour on the ground that it was "only human after all."

Other characteristic Perry phrases that I remember were: "I cyan't awhile" (can't be bothered); "I starves to see it" (said of Lower Farm, and of course he did soon see it, bringing with him prize onions in exchange for a loan of a Massingham); "a noted fact among the common talk" (this one we found useful); "s'bare you could hunt a spider" (of high fields above Shipton); and — once, while dressing for an occasion — "If I could find my best pants, 'ooman, it'd be half my life."

When I last met him he had, some weeks back, fractured a collarbone, which was still causing a "galdy" chafing in the armpit. I was required to "feel the place." "It still knows the weather," he told me, "and finds I when it's wet." We went on to talk of this and that till somehow we drifted round to a mutual acquaintance whose luck was out. "One way and another," I suggested, "she has a lot to put up with." He nodded and pointed his pipe stem at me in emphasis, "Depend 'er do," he said firmly, "depend 'er do."

For the return walk from Wychwood we might take the road that twisted down through Mulberry, if only for a sight of the Neville children or a word (for she had long since forgiven me) with old Mrs. Frost.

My introduction to the Nevilles had been by way of a dish of wild violets set upon a sill in Mulberry Church, where J happened to be "doing the flowers." Someone, it was clear, had done a great deal of picking, for there were at least seven bunches of various sizes and all had been massed in a shallow earthenware dish and then lifted on to the sill to catch the greenish light diffused by the old leaded panes. But what was most remarkable in the flowers, which smelt sweetly, was their colour. They appeared to be wild, for they were smaller than most cultivated kinds, and yet here were not only violet violets but white, blue, purple and some distinctly reddish ones which, as I came to know later, grew on a hidden bank beside larches planted over Saxon graves.

It was the Neville children, I was told, who had gathered them, and their mother the carter's wife who

75

had arranged them and put them on the sill. They prided themselves, these children, on finding the very first (and who more fitted, short and untroubled and sharp-eyed as they were), and their cold little fingers vied in colour with the flowers as they drew them through the frosted March grasses.

I never could decide how many they were "in family." Johnny, the eldest, with his freckles, stood out clearly enough as he shepherded the rest along, tidied their "tramples" to birds' nests and saw to it that the pram didn't run away down Mulberry Hill. I could remember, too, that the other boy was Roddy and the red-haired baby Margareet; but for the rest they were a freckled flock, a charm of small girls, no more distinct in my mind as to name and number than so many goldfinches.

Violets, as I say, happened to be my introduction, but they might equally well have been daisies, since another nice way of theirs was to hang a daisy-chain on a gatepost, in the manner of a gypsy's patteran.

How they all squashed into the smallest cottage in the village I never discovered. In the daytime they were seldom indoors, and it was cheering of a sunny afternoon to see their mother lock the place up and make time to play with them down in the wood. But there was often work for them too, helping "our mum" clean the church and "our dad" stoke its boiler. One day we noticed that one of the girls' hair and eyelashes were singed, and we asked what had happened. "I was by the furnace in church," she explained, "and the flames fled out and singed me." "And at the back too?"

we said. "Yes," she assured us, "the flames fled after me when I ran away."

Barelegged and unhushed they went about their church business while we changed the frontals (an awkward job, like making the Great Bed of Ware) or J arranged the altar flowers, a pleasant task enough except that what she put there was not always to the churchgoers' taste. Mrs. Frost, for instance, deprecated what she called weeds on the altar (wild flowers of any sort) and there was that embarrassing time when Our Lady's Bedstraw (*Galium verum*), foaming in saffron clouds against faded blue hangings, puffed pollen up the congregation's noses and got itself and its sponsors violently disliked. Teazles, too, could be importunate when placed in the nave, for as the choristers swung by they clung to their cassocks and one even stayed the course as far as the pulpit. ("What were those awful clinging things?" J was asked).

But the Neville children, while quite as full of mischief as most, had a zest for country things — flowers and birds, fields and woods and water — which was surely exceptional, judging from the less admirable tastes and pastimes of some of the village children we see to-day. They were too, without being in the least goody-goody, most pleasingly appreciative and responsive — qualities rarer still — as when, for instance, they came to our Christmas party, for which we had planted, in our farm parlour, a young Christmas tree from the wood.

And what, we often wonder, has become of that large and engaging family? For they left the village long

77

before we did and disappeared into the depths or rather, the heights of the Cotswolds, to a remote farm called Trafalgar, which of course was equivalent to translation to another world.

But the two pictures I have now as I think of them are first, of a group of children on the grass about an apple tree, up which a small girl is giving her still smaller sister a "boost." They are there to see "our" owl's nest, and as the very small girl's fair head draws level with the peephole, she bobs back startled. Her face, as she turns to us, is flushed and freckled and delighted. "Cor," says she on a note of wonder, "but hasn't that got big eyes?"

The other picture is of the whole charm, covey or gaggle of children (except for the baby in her pram in the porch) asprawl on Mrs. Chick's much-worn rag rug in front of our fire. There is a tangle of bare legs that don't seem to belong to any child in particular. Chins rest on palms, and for once the whole family — normally in a pleased twitter — is absolutely quiet. Before each lies an open book with every other page a picture . . . They are reading the works of Beatrix Potter.

EVOLUTION OF A DRYAD

Nearer my God to thee . . .
would I knew now
childhood's clear joy to be
high on a bough.
The stoop of beauty's wing

among those skies
sharper delight could bring
then to my eyes.

When the tall cherry tree
took in kind arms
tears, spelling book and me,
hung us with charms
(ear-rings to dangle cool
at a child's ear,
gum like a heather pool,
amber and clear);
swinging with blackbirds there,
truant indeed,
I strangely, suddenly
knew I could read.
I who had come as free
as thieving birds
went from the cherry tree
solemn with words.

Heavy with words I go
slave to their whim,
anxious lest I should show
their beauty dim;
with unenchanted hands
make dull and faint
beauty the cherry tree
taught me to paint.

J. M. W.

CHAPTER
THREE

Evenlode Country nearer Oxford

(I) THE COTTAGE

If this book were an autobiography I should feel bound to dwell on the series of more or less violent, not to say melodramatic incidents which dug us out of Lower Farm, packed J and the baby off to Shropshire and myself to the London Fire Service and eventually brought us together again in Oxfordshire, some sixteen miles nearer Oxford than where we had first settled. But the book is not so intended, and since doubtless the gentle reader's war stories are as good as if not better than the author's, suffice it to hint at the nightmares and skip them in favour of (as I hope) more pleasurable stuff.

Of all the moods in which a prospective house-buyer may find himself, desperation is, I suppose, the least favourable. Considering, then, the state of despair to which living in other people's houses had brought us, no doubt we deserved to be bitten, when we bought this cottage, a great deal more severely than we were.

For the first few weeks indeed it did seem to us both that the bite had been mortal; nor did the smart decrease as we listened to the gloomy ones (common to every village since the time of Job and doubtless before) spreading themselves on the notorious incurability of the various snags and tantrums peculiar to our new home.

"Drain gone wrong *again?*" asked one, eyeing J's worried back from the roadside of our tumbling wall, "I expect you find the bathwater laps back over the floor when you pull the plug out, don't you? Comes back through the wall, doesn't it? Yes, it would do that, always did. Why, often and often I've seen Mrs. B. at it just as you are now, trying to get it to go. Oh yes . . ."

And another, "Fire smoking, did you say?" (quiet chuckle), "know what Mr. and Mrs. B. used to do?" (as if we cared), "Ah, Christmas-time too. Used to fling the door open wide they did, so as everyone could see 'em, and then on with their top coats to sit shiverin' beside it while the smoke billowed out."

Another, trying sincerely to console us, had to admit that when she had glanced into the front room while it was unfurnished she "did just say 'Oh, my God!'" Yet another thought it only kind to warn us that "come harvest" we should inevitably be overrun with mice. And all with one voice united in deploring the "fancy price" we had paid for what after all, but a few hundred years back, must have been run up as a gardener's cottage for less than a hundred pounds.

It was certainly madness to buy a cottage that had not even been glanced at by the woman who was going to live in it, but then they were mad days, days when the desperate were sinking their all in grim little

gardenless boxes in what looked like colonies for lepers
. . . "The sum you mention," my solicitor told me,
"to-day buys nothing. If the place is at all what you say
it is, with gas and electricity and mains water, snap it
up at once without quibble." I took his advice.

Even before she had witnessed the bathwater's trick
of lapping back across the floor or been half choked by
the belching fire, J decided that she disliked the cottage
wholeheartedly. It was too public (plumb in the middle
of the village, between school, pub and church); not
light enough (facing west, its back to the village); and
such little ground as it had looked hopelessly
neglected.

Without much conviction I tried to stress its more
obvious charms; the air of solidity, the sunny Cotswold
stone, the bathroom, the large parlour, the unusual
little corridor upstairs, with two bedrooms leading off
it, the large attic which we would (and did) convert
into a spare room. Then there was a largish stone
outhouse where I might some day have a workroom;
there were the towering chestnuts to look at and our
magnificent neighbour the stone-spired church, not to
mention the little grey village itself on its hill near the
Evenlode, not far from Oxford, which was just where
we had been wanting to be.

It was a pity that while I was talking the noise of
aeroplanes, gravel lorries, and children let out from
school all but drowned my words. To bad drains and
chimneys and the general run of "upsters" the
householder is heir to, both of us, I think, are of
average steadiness. Noise, however, sudden noise,

excessive noise, deliberate, persistent, unnecessary noise is our Waterloo . . . It was decided then and there that we must move by the following spring at latest, even if it meant selling at a considerable loss.

When at this stage we confided in a friend, who is Russian, telling her frankly the full extent of our folly, all she would say, as I thought irrelevantly, was, "How is the furniture fitting in?" I told her it was fitting in magically well. The dresser, after some anxious moments, had taken its stand with exactly an inch to spare. The margin for desks and chests of drawers was about the same. Everything, in fact, was finding its comfortable niche. "In that case," said our friend with finality, "you will stay."

We have stayed, so far, four years.

All that the drain needed was a firm, professional hand. The treatment prescribed by our local builder was far-reaching and fundamental, involving deep trench work by an army of good fellows, all of whom, by a coincidence, took sugar in their tea. And how miraculous it seems still, when the plug is pulled out of the bath, to see the water disappearing and know that (touch wood) it will not surge softly backward as it did before. (To date there has been only one occasion of backsliding, and that when, after a complete stoppage and some backwash, the garden end of the wastepipe disgorged four toads, three adults and one lost-looking juvenile. We could scarcely believe our eyes as, with obvious reluctance, the procession yielded to the rush of water and slowly plopped out.)

All that the chimney needed was rather frequent attention from a sweep who, I am told, has a mahogany leg, a nice face, and always gets his shallots in before Christmas.

As for mice, they might well have overrun us had it not been for J's Better Mousetrap. To look at, it is just another of those tuppenny, break-back affairs of wood and wire, the kind that usually catches only fingers (one suspects they are made *by* mice *for* mice), and yet, uncanny as it seems, for this particular trap the mice almost literally queue. Indeed, when a mouse-plague hits the village, as at threshing time it must, J scarcely has time to turn her back after resetting before snap it goes again, disposing of yet another endearing little creature whose one sin is that it is not house trained, and so cannot help itself to a modest share of the rations without leaving traces offensive to one's senses of cleanliness and smell.

I have examined the trap closely. But no. In an age of self-advertisement, the maker of the Better Mousetrap remains anonymous. Perhaps he dreads a track being beaten to his door. The only words on the trap are "MADE IN ENGLAND," which, of course, should be recommendation enough.

J's own theory . . . But one day I hope to publish a collection of Women's Wonderful Theories, in which hers about the Better Mousetrap will assuredly be one of the first. In the face of all good housewifely instincts (the same that compel her to scrub acres of stone floor and polish obstinate boards) she maintains that a mousetrap should not be scrubbed, that it should in fact be left bloody, until, wholly impermeated, it gets mistaken by the mice for another of their species or even for a kind of super hermaphrodite mouse of double gender appealing irresistibly to one and all.

The obvious weakness is, of course, that to begin with your new trap is as clean as a whistle. How, then, to get it blooded? All must depend at this stage upon bait and setting . . . But I must not digress on such an extensive subject. Suffice it to say that the Better Mousetrap gets its mouse and so saves us from harbouring a cat, an animal which far outdistances the mouse in revolting habits, including, as everyone knows, yowling, slow torture and the killing of birds.

Two minor menaces which the pessimists forgot to mention are clothes-moths and spiders. Of the former, doubtless we get no more than our share, though I sometimes wonder, as I come upon a cloud of them in the attic, how often and how much they make other people worry. "It's the one thing I shall like about heaven," I heard a housewife murmur the other day, "it definitely says *not*." (Matthew vi. 20.)

Of spiders we have, I am certain, some hundreds at least in excess of our quota, and this partly because our predecessors removed all the ceilings, thus exposing to view a kind of joist-tenement which, though doubtless present in most houses, normally remains a cloistered and private mezzanine floor. Not that we object to spiders in themselves. Each one is a miracle, and so of course is every web it weaves. When we first took the cottage we had soft feelings for them. "I should leave a few webs around," one good soul rather needlessly —

85

or was it tactfully — advised, "they catch the flies, you know." A pretty fancy. Generally speaking, only the smallest and least irritating flies are weak and foolish enough to get caught, although the largest spiders (tarantula type) when roused can and will tackle anything.

While we were at tea yesterday, hearing a loud buzz which seemed to come from the shelf marked "POEMS," I found a hairy-legged giant in the act of making a neat, shop-assistant's parcel of a honeybee. The spider had, in fact, dragged the bee down behind the Poetical Works of George Meredith and was quite obviously resentful when I fished it up again with a spoon. As I was trying to de-web the victim, the spider rushed to the top of the book where, with its legs planted firmly in cage formation over the bee's body, it took up an attitude of insolent defiance. What it actually did to the bee I cannot say, but it was lethal, for although I cleaned it and laid it tenderly on a head of bergamot, it would not revive. It may well be that the shock alone was enough.

This morning brings news and evidence of another smaller spider which, thrust out of the bathroom window, rushed back at once to kill and dismember its fellow which had just fallen into the bath . . . Much more of this, thought I, and homo sapiens will begin to show up as a kindly, civilized being.

You will probably know the French spider-rhyme our Russian friend taught us:

Arraignée du matin: chagrin
Arraignée du tantôt: cadeau
Arraignée du soir: espoir

A jingle which gives one, for what it's worth, a new interest in spiders and a two-to-one chance of some degree of good luck. In time one becomes quite good at not seeing a morning spider, though a black one in an empty bath does, I must own, take some missing. A friend, knowing her mother's peculiar horror of spiders, asked her what she did if she saw one while alone in the house. "I stamp on the floor, dear," she said, "which usually makes it run under the piano, and if that fails, I go to bed."

Our bathroom, it is said, was once full of barrels of beer. Deeds have told us little of the cottage's history, nor has local memory taken us far, but it seems certain that the place was once a small tavern or hedgehouse and it was where our predecessors put in bathroom, kitchen and larder that the stock of liquor was kept. (To-day, although the drinkables are missed, a piping-hot bath every evening is almost as enheartening; and there is always The Stook & Sickle just over the way.)

In more recent years the cottage has served as a sweet-shop and slept eleven in an attic we consider just airy enough for two. It was in its sweet-shop days that it was enriched with shelves beneath the front windows to take the jars. At least that is my guess, though our five-year-old differs. He thinks that they were once window-seats and is anxious to prove it. "I must borrow a tape-measure some time," he suggested yesterday, "to see how many people would have sat there in a row, going by the amount that would be wide enough for a bottom."

More recently still, so recently — a mere fifteen years ago — that only the other day we had a caller who expected us to repair his bicycle, the cottage was lived in and its outhouse worked in by our friend Frank Mason, the bicycle man.

"Never know'd such a place for beetles," he told me when I asked what he remembered best. "When we first come there it was springtime and I come home late one night, when the weather was growin' warmer, and lit a candle and — well, you wouldn't believe me if I was to tell you. Beetles? The floor of the front parlour was black with 'em, like a flock o' black sheep and runnin' all ways . . . 'Right,' I said. Next night we sat up, brother and me, and when our Mum asked why, 'We're goin' beetle-huntin',' I said. Flat bits o' wood we had with sticks for handles and we sat very quiet in the dark till all of a sudden I gives the signal and we lights up and lashes out. Well, I never seed s'many in all my life. We kept shovellin' and shovellin' till we had nigh on a barrer-load o' black bodies; but that rid us of 'em every one, and we never had a beetle come near us up there again."

Nor have we seen them in any quantity either. No, all things considered, we were not so very badly bitten when we bought the old place. There is more than charm to it, there is comfort, yes, and when the children are in school, even some quiet. The ruined garden wall has been rebuilt and a sandpit of sorts made for the five-year-old behind it.

He it was who, up to his neck in the Evenlode yesterday, expressed what I had almost been daring to think myself. "Whatever we do," said he, "don't let's ever move our house. This is the nicest place there *could* be for a house, isn't it? By a river and all . . ."

Perhaps it is.

(II) THE GARDEN

Of the opinions freely expressed by the village upon our small garden, none has been more disconcerting than that of our grandest neighbour — "Your miserable little patch" — and none more gratifying than that of perhaps our most modest — "It's a little paradise, isn't it?"

Certainly it is small, consisting of two plots — a square one between the front of the cottage and the churchyard; and a triangular "pecked piece" on the south, which includes a "lawn," Roger's sandpit, a disused well and a potato patch — neither of them nearly as large as a tennis-court.

At this time of year (July) there is scarcely, in either plot, an inch of earth to be seen. The broad beans encroach on the pea rows; a tomato plant has been engulfed by a riot of phloxes; and above the forest of foxgloves and gooseberry bushes which crowd against the wall we share with the churchyard, a few tousled heads of elecampane can just be seen coming up for air.

Viewing all this one June evening, the gardener, who is also the housewife, sighed for a larger garden. "Be a rector," she suggested, "with a huge old rectory and acres of walled garden. Why not?" With Naboth's vineyard and one or two other things in mind, I felt I could not honestly regard this as a call, and said so. However, the debate, off and on, continues. "You see, if we had more space," she pointed out, "we could have bright annuals like nemesia and phlox Drummondii, except, of course," she added irrelevantly, "that Drummondii have no smell, and it seems awful for a phlox not to smell, delicious as they are."

We were standing just then on the little path she had bordered with larkspur. "I took great pains choosing seed from the colours we like," she said, "and cutting out those rather dreary ones; but if they don't come true, of course all my trouble will be wasted. People murmur darkly, you know, about The Bees . . ."

Sure enough, now that the larkspurs have opened there is not one clear pink one among them; what pink there are being liberally streaked with blue. But then gardens do have a tendency to run to one particular colour. With ours it is not blue — that is just the harkback peculiar to larkspur — but yellow. Relax a moment and you have bed upon bed of yellow daisies large and small, from tansy and erigeron to sunflower and elecampane; all good things enough, but one tires of yellow, and — well, with a small garden one has above all things to be firm.

One of the things which influenced me in buying the cottage was the tree-mallow (*Lavatera arborea*) flourishing near the south wall. About ten feet high, it was a cloud of deep pink flowers. (I had seen it before on the cliffs of Wales and Cornwall and regarded it as a wild, sea shrub.) We took the cottage and waited. . . . The "tree" is biennial, and so far all of ours, though swaddled in sacking, have been killed by frost before they could flower. A thing that has puzzled us has been the never-failing supply of tree-mallow seedlings, for since the trees never flower for us, how are they able to drop seed? But the Curator of Kew is helpful here. "Usually," he writes, "it has an abundance of seed which makes it easy of increase, and in view of the fact that you state that plenty of young plants appear to spring from the ground each year, it does seem that at some time or other your plant must have carried seed which has laid dormant in the soil year after year." The gardener, however, though too optimistic to uproot the leafy survivors, agrees that two years is a long time to wait and worry over them, even on the chance of harbouring a pink cloud.

Most people, I expect, know this kind of disappointment. Shall I ever forget my mother's chagrin when, moving to yet another suburban house, she found that the umbrella roses had been uprooted and taken away? "But that's what I *liked* about the place," I hear her say.

On the other hand, what a host of good neighbours and good things, invisible on viewing day, are apt to turn up and more than compensate. It would, of course, be folly to buy a cottage simply because a humming-bird hawk-moth visited the garden or because goldfinches fed on the cornflower seeds near the porch. Yet had we known these things I cannot say that they would not to some extent have influenced us or that we should not have been sorry to forego them.

We watch the hawk moth through binoculars and now and then jot down what we see. On September 16th, for instance, it "methodically visited the campions, the larkspur and the phloxes, its white dots behind chestnut underwings showing very distinctly. J compared its eyes with a bird's and called it 'the nearest thing to a fairy.' When it had done it fairly whizzed out of the garden."

For fruit and vegetables we are very restricted, the more so on account of our predecessors, who not only ran to gooseberry bushes, which all but hem us in and, fruitful as they are, dare us to uproot them, but to that plaguey habit of planting pips.

Bang in the middle of the front patch, where the space can least be afforded, we have an apple tree. "Growed it from a pip!" the old sweetie-shop dear would triumphantly tell her neighbours. And it bears well. Each autumn it is laden with enormous yellow apples which, unless one has a penchant for washleather, are quite uneatable. Each spring, moreover, there is the problem of avoiding it as one sows seed. As a sympathiser, who happened to be a fireman, said, "it's half a row o' peas and then a' apple-tree and then the other half row." It *must* come down.

We do owe to some anonymous predecessor, however, the one good fruit tree, an Early Rivers plum, which *is* early and ripens with most heartening certainty and munificence on the south wall. It is by no means the best plum I have tasted, nor is it large, but

92

for a plum-pie in July, with egg-custard lightly flavoured with laurel, it has my vote and gratitude every time.

Would that I could say the same for the nameless pear which sulks — and no wonder — on the north wall of the stone outhouse. It is a wretched position for it, but as that same fireman-gardener told me, "Whoever done that done right. The plum must have the south wall. The pear must take its chance more in the shade." I am sorry for the pear-tree, though. The half-dozen fruits it gives us yearly are delicious eating; the rest rot and drop off in infancy through lack of sun.

In flowers we both naturally prefer cottagey things, bright, bunchy, old-fashioned things with strong scents; and for their background all the different greens and shapes of herbs: rue, southernwood, bergamot, wormwood, fennel, balm, marjoram . . .

Of lilies two kinds so far — *regale* and *tigrinum splendens* — have taken to our gravel soil; but the gardener is not old enough, so she says, to be successful in growing "madonnas"; and indeed, in our village at least, it is quite easy to pick out the old women's cottages by their dazzling shows of these lilies. One such, whose "madonnas" flower to perfection year after year, takes scissors and carefully snips off every one of their stamens, for she cannot bear the virgin white to be stained with yellow.

When our first Regal Lily bud — a great pink-ribbed affair like a canoe — burst open (and "burst" is the word) Roger, then four, came running in with cheeks as flushed as the flowers. "Mummy's lily's *face!*" he gasped.

93

To Miss Mitford, you remember, tiger lilies were "those fierce and warlike flowers." I wish we had clump upon clump of them, the tawny kinds and the equally fierce pink and white and all roaring more gently than any sucking dove. I wish we could grow *Lilium japonicum* and *Lilium canadense* and *pomponium* and *rubellum* and *cernuum* and *ochraceum* and most certainly *Lilium Davidi*, and of course the charming little purple carillon called Martagon, which grows wild (*sic*) in a certain wood high up in the Cotswolds.

Martagon . . . There comes to mind the day we spent with the Quaker botanist of wild-garden fame, the late Joshua Lamb. His wild garden, where rare orchises got no pampering but were grown in the same dry-looking plot as a mandrake, was remarkable indeed; and the deaf gardener, in his remote thatched cottage, even more so. When I asked if a Martagon Lily grew in his garden, my question, as was their practice, was passed on by his wife. "Hast thou a Martagon Lily in thy garden?" she asked. He shook his head and denied that it could be called "wild."

Talk drifted, over the teacups, from flowers to rings, Mrs. Lamb agreeing with J that they were, on the whole, a waste of money. "Yet you wear one yourself," J said, "but perhaps that is for wantonness?" At this our hostess laughed and her husband cupped his hand for a share of the joke. "Yon damsel saith," his wife told him, "'for wantonness'!"

So much for memory's roots to the Martagon Lily. At the other end of the scale, it would be exciting to have a shot at growing *Lilium giganteum*, "that noble

94

lily of huge growth, the flower stems six to ten feet high terminated by a huge raceme, one to two feet in length, of about a dozen long, nodding, fragrant flowers, white tinged with purple." And indeed, when I read in Robinson that "it is one of the hardiest lilies and gives very little trouble," I felt encouraged to try. But now comes the snag. "The soil must be deep and well drained, and must consist of sandy peat and leaf-mould, strengthened by a little rich loam and plenty of rich manure. Years sometimes elapse before the tufts of foliage send up bloom." Thank you, Mr. Robinson, I think I will file that away with my favourite recipe which calls for large quantities of cream and brandy and a dozen eggs.

It was Jefferies, I think, who said that even if there be no heaven, it still remains to the glory of man to have imagined one; and it is a little like that perhaps with *giganteum*. The mind's eye looks up longingly at the huge raceme, and then, without by any means abandoning the project or dismissing it as for ever unattainable, drops again to concentrate on the muck-rake. And even that has its technique, or at least the muck has. "Old Mrs. L. has promised to let us have some," the gardener told me, "for the cucumbers. But it must be well rotted old horse, so be ruthless and refuse all worthless imitations."

As I trundled the barrow down the village street I kept repeating to myself, "Well-rotted old horse, well-rotted old horse"; and yet when old Mrs. L. so kindly ousted the calves from the byre so that I might "get at the good stuff," I hadn't the heart (or the courage) to say my piece . . . "It may do," J said doubtfully, seeing what I had brought; but it didn't, and I knew only too well, when I saw the leaves of the cucumbers wilting, that I should have been ruthless and insisted on being given the freedom of the stable.

From time to time I pass on to the gardener such floral oddments and unconsidered trifles as come my way. Our thyme and yellow rockrose, for instance, come from Cotswold verges. (I was on my way back from Strawberry Jim's.) Our achillea and sops-in-wine are from a wartime billet. The tree-lupin I brought as the smallest and youngest member of a great frothing yellow family in a Shropshire wood. Our tobacco flowers were given me, in fearful secrecy, by the head gardener of a London park. Of plant-grabbing, let me hasten to add, we think little and of rarity-grabbing still less. There are times, however, when every gardener is able and glad to give and whether it be on account of the grace that goes with giving, at all events with us these gifts always "take" and flourish and remind us of the giver. When the plant is wild it is, of course, up to the gardener to help himself only where there is abundance and where natural growth will soon fill the gap. In our garden there are three specimens of *Fritillaria meleagris* . . .

For many springs now we have made pilgrimage to the William Morris country to see fritillaries flowering in the water-meadows. In the old days there would come a postcard from a farmer's wife, with two words on it:

SNAKES HEADS

and we would know that to see them at their best we must not delay. Only a few of the flowers grew in that particular field. We had not the least notion of the riches hidden but a few miles off until one day a chance acquaintanceship led to our being sworn to secrecy and conducted a long, rambling way along a towpath beside a disused canal.

There are still in the remoter parts of England paths, like Kipling's road through the woods, which "only the keeper knows," the gamekeeper or it may be the lock-keeper, where the sedge-warbler's eggs are safe from fingers and the kingcups and irises never fall into gypsies' baskets. Such a path was this towpath, and one felt very much the intruder as one forced a way through willow and ash and hawthorn, to come suddenly upon a vast, empty, dripping-rusty lock.

Then on across fields (we would never have found the way without our guide), to a row of willows with a rookery in them, and on again until suddenly, beyond the next hedgerow, the flowers were there.

My first fantastic impression was that it had been raining Victoria plums, which now lay thickly among the short grass of the large meadow. Most of the flowers were wine-coloured and chequered, a few creamy white. We picked some — it is no sin: there are millions — and they rattled drily together, giving out a faint smell suggestive of *bêtes fauves*.

Slowly as we went, and to hurry in such a place would be as ungracious as to run through the Elysian

Fields, we found it difficult to avoid treading on the flowers. Some plants were double-headed, some bore darker and finer flowers than the rest; some, in bud, were like snakes; others, when the sun shone through them, were more like lanterns or upturned glasses miraculously full of wine.

As we wandered back towards the lock and the towpath and turned for one last look at the glowing myriads, I thought of how we would return with our guide again and again. As things turned out, we were to find our way alone; and this we do each spring, ever grateful for the flowers and for her kindness (she died young) in sharing them.

Every garden worthy of the name is a secret garden, inasmuch as the gardener sees more to each plant than does the casual observer. Who, for instance, would guess the origin of those five flourishing balsam poplars at the far (but not very far) end of the lawn? They were rescued as dry twigs from the rubbish-heap of a fruit farmer, whose wife cannot share our enthusiasm for the balsam smell. With us they have done almost too well, and are already overdue for thinning. "I'm not going to do anything about them till the spring," the gardener has just announced, "when they're all in bud they will smell wonderful. I know it's madness, but every spring I've longed for somebody to send me some and now I shall have a little forest of my own."

And that primula popping up on its comically tall, slim stem beside them to hang a delicate-looking head of frail, yellow bells? That is *Primula Florindæ*, "one of the tallest of the species, with gigantic stems of sweetly-scented sulphur yellow hanging bells. . . . It is the crown of the gardener's achievement to behold its luscious, ample heads on stout, inflexible stems." So says Mansfield. And yet J is proud of her frail *Florindœ* too, as well she may be, having brought it as seed from a wildish part of Blenheim, where it was looking rather more gigantic and luscious. Once it has recovered from the shrinking of its purlieus and has gathered strength, it will yet, so the gardener believes, prove the crown of her achievement.

For myself, my favourite outlook is from the attic, of a still June evening, with perhaps a blackbird chinking in the distance to emphasize the general quiet. The red-and-white flag droops from its mast beside the spire and, as I watch, little Miss M., carrying the huge and beautiful North key, hurries through the churchyard on her way to lock the church for the night. The garden, as I look down on it, glows with pink sweet-williams, blue lupins, anchusa, red rose, gaillardia, pinks, cornflowers, pansies, the regal lily in pink bud, aquilegia, stocks . . .

Later, of an August evening when the cottage smells of pinks and the phloxes are out, we see them in the light that streams out from our windows and through the open door. The phloxes are all colours — pink and white, red and white, mauve and white — and of one clean old-fashioned powdery smell. As we watch, the humming-bird hawk moth, on an unusually late forage, is suddenly there to probe them, which it does, silently and methodically, and as suddenly disappears. The tiger lily with its tiers of buds and flowers looks more like a candelabra than ever. We keep the door propped open so that we can see it and the path which runs into the darkness towards the church and might, for all we can see, go on for ever.

So let us leave it: a vast, limitless garden, of the earth earthy and yet for some with more than a hint of heaven; for if we wait for the cold light of morning, someone with no nonsense about him is almost certain to call it "that miserable little patch."

(III) THE CHURCH

When you are yet some miles from our village which stands, amid flattish river country, upon a small hill, you see north-west of Oxford a tall, stone spire. I have known it black as Nelson's column, I have known it golden, and I have known it from half a mile off, on a pale spring day, seem part of the sky itself.

As I look up at the spire now (and from Church Cottage one is bound to look that way often) it seems to me that there cannot be another like it, no, not even in the City of Spires itself; that one such miracle is as much as can reasonably be expected and that nowhere else in the world could anything quite so perfectly proportioned and altogether felicitous be found.

Within, as you stand on a beam in the belfry and gaze up into the eight-sided cone, dimly lit by stone-hooded slits, not a single cross-bar nor any kind of obstruction checks the eye as it follows the pale stone to the far apex.

How was it done? What daring architect conceived the notion of transmuting Cotswold stone into airy lightness? And who were the masons skilled enough to make stone live?

A friend, who lives near a house with a plaque on it, tells me she has never been in, although her favourite poet once lived there and the place is now open for all to see. "They'd never let me take it in for myself," she explained, "there'd be sure to be someone there to tell me all about it."

So it is that I feel about our spire; and until someone insists on disillusioning me I shall go on, to my heart's content, imagining how it was raised. To-day, for instance, may favour something Heath Robinson, involving ingenious engines held together with knotted bootlaces; whereas to-morrow may see squadrons of stout angels and archangels bringing block after block and deftly laying them, while a cloud of hovering cherubs stands by with the stone crown and the winds' initials; and St. Peter, to whom (with St. Paul) the church is dedicated, brings up the rear with his great golden bird.

Angels and archangels may have gathered there,
Cherubim and Seraphim thronged the air . . .

I forget who it was who told us that we had "quite a nice church," though I well remember the visiting craftsman (a clock-maker) who, after gazing for some time at the spire in silence said with feeling, "I must come again and *look* at that." St. Peter's is, in fact, what a church should be: glorious, and to make it so craftsmen from the twelfth century onwards have given

101

of their inspired best. And yet for all its nobility — the sheer, soaring grandeur of the fluted pillars, the stirring loveliness of the faded screen — there is nothing gloomy about it, little that could be called austere. Rather there is much to remind one that mason and carpenter were men; much that is human and endearing.

For example, beside the one jarring feature, the east window (a Victorian gewgaw on which some crude Philistine spread himself), one sees from outside nothing less homely than a bedroom window. True, there is now no bedroom behind it, nor even a floor; but there used to be, and here it was, so the Rector tells me, that the visiting priest from some far parish would spend the night.

The first thing he saw as he looked out over the gravestones would be Church Cottage; and as I see him now, he looks earnestly, one might almost say yearningly, towards it, rather as old Paddy, the farmer's sheepdog, looks up at our kitchen window. And sure enough, as the priest watches, a child, bearing before him something covered with a white cloth, leaves the cottage and slowly, with cautious tread, makes his way through the grassy churchyard to disappear into the north porch, where the door has been left open.

For a moment it might almost seem, as the child carries the covered vessel to the high altar, that he has in some unorthodox way been entrusted with the Host; but instead of pausing and genuflecting he turns north through an archway and climbs the narrow steps to the priest's room. The priest takes the steaming meal from the boy, and with some feeling blesses both; nor does he fail to bless cook and cottage and all within it, "now and for ever." . . .

It is in the north porch, above the Norman doorway, that a jovial St. Peter, a huge key over each shoulder, sits enthroned, the lamb of St. John at his left hand, St. Mark's curly-maned lion at his right, all vigorously done in stone. So far so good. But whose is the restraining hand stealing in from outside the picture to pat, stroke, or get a grip of the unruly lion? The crisply-chiselled, eight-hundred-year-old fingers are, one would say, in the act of stroking; and yet there is about the hand as a whole a strong suggestion of II Corinthians v. 14.

It is yet another of those minor mysteries which set a man guessing and wondering, or alternatively, worrying himself and a pile of old reference books, according to type.

There is less mystery, but as much appeal to the little peephole window in the ringers' room in the tower. Casually, in that dusty, informal place of ropes and ladders, you glance through the window, expecting to see beams or perhaps stone tiles. Instead you find yourself looking straight down to the high altar, far down as to the foot of a cliff, so far that cross, candles, frontals, all are encompassed within those few inches of dull glass. From the body of the church one sees far more clearly and precisely the same scene, without, as it were, seeing it half so well.

As for the ringers, they are a friendly lot, even to making us welcome in the ringing-room. On the June evening I think of, J took a broom with her and got busy, while their captain brushed aside quite a pile of hazel-nut shells to make a place for her on the bench.

"Boys or squirrels?" she asked, and "Boys," she was told, "last autumn . . . Like to come up and have a look at the bells?"

So up we go (with never a word of course of our having been there before), once more to admire them and, still more, the dimly seen interior of the spire . . . Having climbed so far, we cannot resist going out on to the leads, even though it means turning one's body into a corkscrew and acquiring a kind of cobweb-toupet . . .

In spite of the axes that have lately been busy it still looks elm country, with woods (Blenheim and Wytham) on the horizon, and with here and there a willow to mark the twists of the Evenlode, in the middle distance, as it nears the Thames. Close at hand I am pleased to see that even a seraph's eye view allows the vegetable rows in our garden to be straight and, by a coincidence, strictly parallel with the old gravestones beneath us.

And so back to the ringing-room, where all five ringers have arrived and are ready for the practice. "Is it get up and go through or get up and stop?" Captain asks them. "Get up and stop," pipes Treble, a small man, nervous. "Get up and stop it is, then," agrees Captain, "we're all out of practice," and spitting on his hands he seizes the striped sally and takes his stance, one unlaced boot a little before the other. (Captain is tall and lean, about fifty, with an air of knowing what he's about. The others look tense: he is relaxed.)

There is a great clash and then another and another as all five heave on the ropes to feel the bells and get them up, so that for a minute discord flies out over the quiet fields. This is the bells' time, and for a while the ringers give them their heads. Yet underlying the clamour you hear Tenor (Captain's bell) steadying, calling them to order; and sure enough in a little a steady rhythm sets in.

But just as all seems well and the ringers in stride there is a sudden "Stand!" from Captain and the sound falls off and dies. "Right through now?" he asks. "Ah, but what if I mistake?" demurs Treble. "Follow your table and you can't go wrong," Captain tells him, pointing to columns of figures on the wall, "but keep orf the red numbers, them's mine." So sallies are grasped again and serious work begins.

Number Three, a young blacksmith, looks cheerfully confident now, as who would not with biceps rising into hillocks beneath the snowline of rolled sleeves as he strains on the rope. But for style we look to Captain, erect, manifestly at ease, his sally shooting through the ceiling with a convulsive wriggle to vanish completely, as does none of the others, at every alternate stroke. I have to watch it.

Again the bells cease, and "Where's young Bob?" someone asks. "Dunno," says another; "he'll come if he hears us though." And swift on his cue Bob enters, slipping in quietly from the spiral stair. He is sixteen, fair, bronzed, aglow with health. But ah no, he couldn't take a rope, not up to it, he says. (Nonsense, we can all see you're itching to.) Five voices insist and at last, still protesting he'll never do it, he is persuaded. "You'll do it," says Captain, "you've done it afore, now haven't you?" "Ah," agrees Bob doubtfully as he takes over Treble, "but I forgets, see?"

For the third time the bells ring out and for a round or two all goes well. For Bob, though, you can see it's fearful concentration, with arms strained, lips parted and every now and then a wild glance over the shoulder as though he sees Time overtaking him . . . Looks are exchanged. Bob's bell is out of control now, the ringing in chaos. "*Stand!*" roars Captain, and then, "What's the matter, Bob?" Bob is confused. "Shoulda rung that bit twice, eh?" "Ah, that you should." "I needs more practice, see?" "Come, try again then." . . .

At last all goes sweetly and one pictures some ancient campanologist in a distant village nodding approval.

Of a morning if it isn't the barnyard cockerel it is often a bell that wakes us: the deep, polite invitation (how on earth do people get up so early?) followed by the fussy insistence of the five-minuter. We glance up at the weathercock to see what it "bodes." ("Know what I bodes?" the village Jeremiah asked me yesterday, "I bodes thunder.") It is a handsome bird, much perched on by starlings which Tom, who brings the milk and is something of a wag, maintains it "hatches out." It has even been known to take the fancy of the Sunday Boys, whose airgun has left its mark, like a rusty penny, on its tail. And legends crowd about it with the winds . . .

How, for instance when the steeplejacks brought it down for cleaning they carried it into the taproom of

The Stook & Sickle, where beak and tail touched opposite walls. And of course the oldest weathercock legend of all — that it stands for the fickleness of St. Peter — still persists in spite of the preference of most of us to remember the Rock.

It is no legend that this church was once an official place of pilgrimage: you can see the crosses carved by the pilgrims on the door-jambs. And how many of those pilgrims, I wonder, having come so far and found perfection, must have longed to remain, to live in the precincts, with the spire the first thing seen at waking, and the east window aglow as after compline they went to bed?

Matins, as a rule, is well attended, and if one's attention should wander, it would not be the Rector's fault . . . But how I envy those stoics able to sit for an indefinite period on a hard pew, its back kicked, it may be, by a bored and fidgety schoolboy — and still concentrate on the address. Or those again who have somehow managed to mortify not merely the flesh but the whole of the nervous system, so that when a fifteenth-century pulpit of priceless workmanship is seen to be quivering on its stem, they ignore it, and are still, in their unrufflable calm, all ears for the last syllable of parson's saw.

Such, in fact, was the situation last Sunday. Treated to a glare like a blue-piled thunderloft the child, I was happy to see, quailed and stopped kicking; but the pulpit went on quivering and try as I would, I could not but tremble for it too. The preacher, a visitor, was aged and probably nervous. At all events he clutched at the edge of the pulpit like a mouse in a wineglass, till at one time I thought the whole thing must topple over. Not that he was corpulent (I long to see a full-blown but careful bishop overflow it), but our pulpit is small, a made-to-measure affair for the smaller parsons of a distant day.

As things turned out, I need not have worried; for as he warmed to his theme the visitor threw off nervousness, left the pulpit alone and gave an address such as few who were there will forget. Shrewd old sage that he was, he had kept the good wine till the last, so that just as we were beginning to nod there came of a sudden, from that fragile old wineglass of a pulpit, stuff that was strong and heady and all the better for keeping.

And yet would it, I wonder, have tasted so good in less lovely surroundings? It is a poor sort of faith that cannot triumph over circumstance, and if our magnificent church vanished overnight and we woke to a tin chapel, I suppose we might somehow, in time, if we stayed that long, learn to love it . . .

But what a nightmare thought! I look out hurriedly — yes, it is still there, the setting sun gilding the weathercock which little Miss M., who keeps poultry, calls The Bird. There she hurries again now, St. Peter's guardian, armed with his great key, as though if the church were not locked promptly at sundown the Devil might slip in and spend the night there. How scrupulous she is! How nimble and methodical! "Lock up chickens and ducks . . . Lock up church . . ." One imagines her ticking the jobs off on her fingers as she does them — "Hang up key . . . Let out cat . . . Lock up cottage . . . Bed."

(IV) THE CHURCHYARD

In the days when, within fairly generous limits, people could live where they wanted, few chose houses that looked on to churchyards. For most of us the business of travelling hopefully is quite difficult enough without constantly being reminded of what our perishable part must expect when it arrives.

There were those, of course, whose calling or parents' calling gave them no option but to be "girt about with the graveyard," the Brontës among them, and what a heartbreaking prospect that bleak Haworth churchyard was! May Sinclair refers to "tombstones grey and naked, set so close that the grass hardly grows between them." Mrs. Gaskell writes of "a dreary, dreary place, literally paved with rain-blackened tombstones," and goes on to tell us that Charlotte was by no means indifferent to its gloom. In short, no woman liked it; and I doubt if any man, with the possible exception of old Mr. Brontë, did either.

But there is of course another side to the picture, and it is this sunnier, grassier, more sheltered and altogether more cheerful side that we at Church Cottage have the luck to face.

Beginning with the big advantage of that weathered and lichened Cotswold sandstone which merges into its background as only native can, and continuing without one abomination in white marble, we have the added blessings of box and juniper and golden yew, and of grass and wild flowers allowed to do pretty much as they like.

There will always be some, of course, to shake their heads over the wildness of it and call it a disgrace; but even they could hardly deny that the effect is restful, and for us, divided from it by only a low, mossy wall, it seems like a wild extension of our garden. And it is in fact a quite remarkably popular sanctuary for birds.

Not that a bird can ever feel perfectly safe from its fellows — a starling was carried off screaming from a box-bush by a sparrow hawk, before our eyes, during tea the other day — but at least the children don't go "pulling nesties" in the churchyard, and this the birds seem to know.

As a schoolboy I made it a point of honour to find each season more birds' nests than anyone else. (It was not difficult. Competition, for one thing, was never more than lukewarm, nor was tree-climbing as popular as organized games.) Nowadays I don't find half as many, and if I put failure down to the kindly wisdom which comes with maturity and teaches one not to disturb little birds, well, that is my affair, even though I may have spent some time on my knees peering up into the fastnesses of a bramble bush, in vain search of a bullfinch's nest, before coming to any such complacent conclusion.

In the case of the spotted flycatcher, which I knew to be nesting this summer not very many yards from our front door, I must own to a churchyard-wide search, not excluding the rectory drive where I finally ran it to earth, or rather to tree, for it was fixed, somewhat precariously, to the trunk of a chestnut. While in search of it — and here is yet more ammunition for the worthy Never-Disturbers — I inadvertently put off our friendly robin, sitting on a late clutch cleverly hidden within the very heart of a churchyard yew.

The churchyard bullfinch, on the other hand, showed me her nest herself — flitting, twig in beak, into a yew bush while I watched through the embrasured slit in the north porch — and I cannot think that it was our fault that, to our grief, she deserted after laying four eggs. Rather, if it was that she found the world too much with her, blame must be laid at the rectory door, for it is unquestionably due to the new rector that traffic through the churchyard and the west door, near which she nested, has so greatly increased.

All other nesters in the sanctuary, however, from the mistle-thrush in the lime tree to the goldcrest in the yew ("a wonderfully neat hammock of moss, lichens and cobwebs," as Coward says, "with eggs looking like children's comfits"), have, so far as I know, got away with it; not forgetting the greenfinch at the top of the biggest box-bush and the goldfinch whose young ones, tossed up and down in their frail nest on the extremity of a chestnut twig, looked and sounded for all the world like a party of excited children, whistling and singing and shouting to keep their courage up, in an absurdly small boat caught in a mountainous sea.

Many a bird, nesting elsewhere, makes the churchyard part of its "daily walk and ancient neighbourhood." A green woodpecker, for instance, calls regularly for ants, while its relative, the greater-spotted, clings to a tombstone and wonders whether the moss may be worth a peck. It is usually from the churchyard evergreens that we hear the first spring-cascade of the chaffinch, and as the season advances we soon have quite a choir: chiff-chaff and willow-warbler, dunnock and wren, mistle-thrush, blackbird, and that tiresome song-thrush which says nothing but "chick-weed"; goldfinch and goldcrest; greenfinch and linnet; wood-pigeon and turtle-dove, and of course the cuckoo, searching high and low for the wagtail's nest which is not in the churchyard at all but in the ivy of the farmhouse next door. Kestrels scream as they chase each other round the spire. Jackdaws wheel up there (their echoing clatter reminding one of sea cliffs and ruins); as do martins and swallows, hunting late into the summer evening . . .

And still more visitors come and go between us, some uncommon, like the marbled white butterfly which reached our elecampane by way of the churchyard grasses; some common — like the dragonfly I watched through binoculars, its long "tail" a black-and-white and duck-egg blue totem-pole — and none the less welcome.

One day last autumn, when wasps were being so aggressive as to be in danger of losing for ever a couple of staunch human supporters, J, acting on some ingenious person's hint, took offensive action, and, after one or two vain and dangerous attempts, succeeded in lightly knotting a length of scarlet silk round one of their admirable waists. She then let the wasp go out of the front room, hoping, of course, to follow it as it made for its nest. After some slight hesitation and stalling, the wasp with the crimson streamer was well away. Indeed, I had to run to keep up with it, and almost before I realized it I had jumped the churchyard wall. But this would not do. The wasp, after a short rest on a grave, took off and disappeared behind a boxbush, where I declined to follow. The insect, like the birds, had sought sanctuary, and it would hardly be seemly, I felt, to go chasing it over the green mounds, however just the cause.

A walk round the churchyard is apt to be humbling, if only to make one realize what a newcomer, what an interloper one is when brought up against the long-rooted sojourn of one's neighbours. People who have seemed mere settlers have forbears here and have had for generations. Even the meteoric Sunday Boys, roaring up and down the village street on what sound like engines propelled by rockets, even these have their indigenous roots, as is seen from the surname of two of them on a tomb dated 1813.

A great many of the more recent stones bear the family name of a local farmer, now a very old man. Indeed, the first four crosses you see, as you turn from latching the oak-paled gate, commemorate his mother and father and two other relatives, all of whom died from typhoid in the April of 1878. "Father was seventeen at the time," his daughter told us. "He found himself with six children to look after and there would have been a seventh if my grandmother had

113

lived another three months." Nor was it his fault that two of the little girls soon afterwards followed their parents. One of them was drowned while picking flowers beside the Evenlode, the other thrown out of a pony-trap when the pony shied.

That is part of the story that ended with those four stone crosses; but what of all these nameless green mounds; this one, for instance, with the neat little round box-bush at its head? Every now and then — on this July evening, for example, when the church is still heavy with summer heat and the scent of lilies — the anonymous mound wears a small bunch of cut flowers (just now it is mauve phloxes with one short foxglove in among them). Who puts them there? Who trims the box-bush? Who is buried there? Without the least inclination to pry, one cannot help wondering. But it is just another secret in a garden of secrets; for no garden is more mysterious than this.

I have said that there is nothing gloomy about the place, and yet we have two memorials — one the beautifully-lettered casket-tomb to Ralph Reade; the other the almost illegible Parson Denison tablet within the church — which at first glance seem positively sinister, the Reade tomb being garnished with skull and crossbones and bat's wings, while the Denison tablet has as its tailpiece a realistically carved winged skull.

In my ignorance, I tried to imagine (a) a parishioner sufficiently eccentric, not to say ghoulish, to leave orders for such things; (b) a morbid-minded mason; (c) shocked relatives faced with the dilemma of either thanking and paying the perpetrator or risking his offence not only for life but perhaps after it, when rancour and umbrage might well blossom forth in shapes ugly as the Devil and lasting as stone itself.

Reference to the Bodleian, however, showed how very wide of the mark I had been and taught me yet again the folly of guesswork.

"As to the skulls and crossbones, hour-glasses, coffins, spade-picks, torches reversed, found on the decorative panels on Elizabethan and Jacobean tombs," writes Katharine Esdaile in her admirable "Monuments in English Churches," "they are in complete accordance with the spirit of the age as it expressed itself in literature on page after page of Shakespeare and his contemporaries. Even the winged skull," she goes on, "had its lesson: Death on the wings of Time, as an eighteenth-century guidebook explains. It is almost always placed below some symbol of immortality, such as a cherub or flowers. Life, not extinction, is the message of such works." And sure enough, when I came to examine these things again I found on the same panel as the bones and bat's wings symbols of redemption and resurrection, while frisking about the upper parts of the other eighteenth-century tablet (the winged skull one) I discerned no fewer than four frankly triumphant cherubs.

As to the possibility of a morbid mason, however, I must in self-defence mention that I was not utterly at sea, Mrs. Esdaile referring in another of her fascinating books on this subject ("English Monumental Sculpture Since the Renaissance") to a mason, then believed to be C. G. Cibber, with "a love of the morbid amounting almost to a mania, which his patrons did not always share."

Far more pitiful than morbid is our one rhyming epitaph, within the church, to Mary Smith, who died in 1813, and is buried "with two female children." (She was the wife of a curate who was a Fellow of St. John's.) It runs thus:

> Snatch'd hence and only shew'd to human life
> Here lies the perfect pattern of a Wife
> With whom the state of wedlock had no woes
> But when she perish'd in a Mother's throws.
> Vertue like hers need fear no sudden fate:
> They only die too soon who live too late.

Outside, in the churchyard, the chief emblem and keynote, other than the cross, is the cherub, and — seeing that it stands for immortality and is, in the right hands, a creature of charm and cheerfulness, for all its obscure ancestry and oddly truncated being — what could be happier? On every side here one sees flocks and charms and coveys of them. Usually it is one fat-faced cherub with ringlets, heading a stone; but sometimes there are two, though their wings tend to get in each other's way. On some stones the expression is gay, even very gay; on others they look severe and disagreeable and altogether unchildlike. At not a few it would be easy to poke fun — far easier than sculpting an engaging-looking cherub for oneself. Indeed, although, even allowing for weathering, the features on most of these stones seem crude, the *wings* are almost always convincing, that is to say, to all appearances trustworthy and serviceable. (Would this be due to long practice with doves and angels?)

Not long ago in a country mason's workshop I came across the modern counterpart: a new, uncommissioned gravestone with this same cherub motif — but with what a difference! "There is a refinement about the early cherubs," noted my father in his *Old English Clocks*, "that is wanting in the cruder copies by later makers." Most certainly there was little refinement here. I saw a couple of bloated cheeks, dropping fatness and half buried in a ruff of coarse feathers, while below them there obtruded what appeared to be a turgid stomach, much elongated, designed, as I supposed, to carry the epitaph. I could not share the old mason's surprise that the stone had not been jumped at, though I suppose that for an out and out glutton, it would be just the thing, with, of course, some suitable tag . . .

Here lies a man who put his stomach first.
His mind fared poorly but his soul fared worst.
or
A part was greed; the greater part was thirst
or as you will . . .

It was, in short, a most clumsy piece of work with nothing attractive or desirable to it. Had it been otherwise, the vague dream of squeezing my mortal self one day into our overgrown acre — a winged cherub over my head and other winged creatures nesting here and there — might have been indulged in to the extent of placing an order. As it was, that was out of the question; and besides, our leafy, grassy, feathery churchyard was long since full.

All things considered, perhaps one should give another thought to cremation. After all, one might still in some unfrightening and viewless form return to find the birds' nests (more adept at this than the cuckoo), and watch the dragonflies. And in the meantime it is pleasant to haunt the place, at odd moments, in the flesh; very pleasant to listen to the goldcrest tinkling away, even in the rain, from that yew tree, and watch the martins wheeling and hunting up there above the weathercock, very pleasant indeed.

Oh yes, even when your cottage faces a graveyard, even perhaps partly because of it, it's good to be alive . . . It surely is.

(V) THE VILLAGE

While the church is our main point of focus, the bedroom and living-room windows all facing west, Church Cottage has in the back of its head three eyes (the windows of kitchen, larder and bathroom), thanks to which no cottager of average curiosity and alertness need go for one minute poorly informed on contemporary village life.

The grey-roofed village itself, on its little hill, is good to look upon, small and compact; and these back windows of ours, giving on to the village street and The

118

Stook & Sickle, afford what house-agents call "an unrivalled view" of all that is going on.

Often when you look out of the kitchen window your glance is met by a steady stare from the questioning brown eyes of a large woolly dog, "with a broad grin and his ears twitched up," as our five-year-old has described him. "Is it wrong of me," sighed the cottager's wife this morning, "to be tired of his staring at me like that?" It is Paddy, the farmer's lame sheepdog, who insists on taking the place of a dustbin and looks to us for an unfailing supply of snacks, or in other words — words I have seen chalked up outside a Parisian café — *restoration à toute heure*.

It's a wise dog that keeps his eye glued to one of the best cooks in the village; and indeed everything that comes out of that kitchen I find restorative, be it only the cook's daily reports of village life.

In yesterday's high wind, for instance, she was just in time to see our *Oxford Times* disappearing under old Mother Carey's apron. "Hi!" she called, startling the old dame into dropping it. ("Give her her due," J added, "she did think it was an old paper that would do nicely for her fire, but you do have to be *quick* in this village.")

It was this same Mother Carey, usually in black mushroom hat, velvet blouse, patched apron and boots, whom J encountered at the pub corner, one still, dark evening, gingerly carrying a jug of beer in one hand and a *lighted candle* in the other. "Ah, my dear," she muttered as she passed, "it's the corners as does yer," and she vanished into her burrow of a cottage, flame and drink still intact. She is much troubled, poor woman, by the rheumatics, picked up, ironically enough, in the damp wash-houses of ancient Bath. She is a champion wood-gatherer, but she cannot read, and when it came to bread rationing, "They all keeps on at me about bread," she complained, "till me brains comes out o' me ears and I has to bide away from 'em. I had two loaves a week and I still has two loaves a week . . ."

When we first came to the village Mother Carey was devoting her life to a sick cat so strangely afflicted that it was compelled to put its tongue out at all the world, and keep it out, wherever it went. After, as I imagine, a good deal of trial and error, Mother Carey discovered that the one thing the cat appreciated, the one form of treatment to ease its distress, was to be lifted on to the rounded top of a neighbour's gate, there to sprawl, legs a-dangle, tongue protruding, like something left over from a witches' sabbath. Thenceforth the cat-lover's duty was clear. True, finding the brute would often mean an exhaustingly thorough yet not entirely uninteresting search of adjacent gardens, and the ungrateful puss swore horribly when it was caught; but Mother Carey stood no nonsense, and as for the neighbour with the medicinal gate, hers was surely the advantage, for don't people pay to have gargoyles on their houses and deformed manikins on toadstools on their lawns?

Even this treatment, however, and all Mother Carey's devotion could not check the disease which, after some months of lingering, to the grief of its

120

protectress but the relief of the village, carried the cat off, tongue and all, to another place where the gates may or may not be pearly.

But of all the animals seen from our kitchen window — cats, dogs, sheep, goats, donkeys, horses urged on by Italians, cows herded by Germans, and so on — none has been more surprising than the polecat ferret which J, in the midst of cooking, noticed huddling along down the lane that runs beside the pub. After questing around for a minute it seemed to make up its mind and hurried under the door marked GENTLEMEN. But that wouldn't do. It soon appeared again, sniffing and huddling and running around as though it wanted to go wild but had forgotten how.

It had just vanished again when out of the front door of the pub stepped a tough-looking countryman with something on his mind. At least he appeared preoccupied as he took up his bicycle and began wheeling it down the street. "Hi!" J called out to him. (There are times, rare occasions, when it is needful to shout "Hi!" from our cottage. This was the second of them) — "Do you keep a ferret?" The man looked astounded. For a moment he couldn't locate the voice, and when he did he kept his gaze fixedly on the stranger and gave her a confident "Yes," while at the same time reaching with a brown hand towards a small and distressingly thin looking sack which dangled from his handlebar . . .

Never, the watcher tells me, did man's face fall with more comic abruptness than when his groping fingers discovered no softly yielding bulge. However, he soon recaptured the ferret and it gave no trouble at all. I suppose that for all the swaying of the smelly little sack, the smell and the rough feel of it would be familiar and the ferret glad enough to be back in it, swinging along with its absentminded master towards hutch and home.

It is hardly to be wondered at that with her cook's-eye view of it — which I don't altogether envy, a man never being so inescapably chained to his desk as a woman to her stove — and her various errands at cottage and farmhouse, J should know the village far more intimately than I do. Indeed, she ought to be writing this chapter even if it meant ruining a good meal. To-day, for instance, the generosity of the village and the impossibility of keeping pace with it is the current theme. "I send Roger with a basket of plums for Mrs. P., for some little service," she has been saying, "and back comes the basket full of tomatoes. I go down to Hester's with plums and find she has already started out with a bowl of loganberries for us."

Occasionally, as I sit writing in the attic, looking vainly perhaps to the weathercock for inspiration, a few words of conversation come drifting up. The other day, for instance, the caller was Mrs. Fairbanks, the same who, after our first Monday's residence, congratulated her new neighbour on her full clothes line. ("Your washing looks nice, Mrs. Green, really it does, much nicer than we'd expected") — and the topic: window-cleaners . . .

Mrs. F.: "I've had the window-cleaners."

J.: (*enviously*): "Oh, have you? I saw them at the rectory, but didn't dare ask them."

Mrs. F.: "Oh yes, Mrs. Mundsley-Potter had 'em and I thinks, 'My money's as good as hers,' and so I asks 'em to come over."

J.: "Inside and outside too?"

Mrs. F. (*shocked*): "Oh, only outside, of course!"

J.: "But why not inside too? Why not make a job of it?"

Mrs. F.: "What, have Strange Men in the bedroom? Oh, Mrs. Green, I *am* surprised at you!"

It was the window-cleaners who were so vociferously at work in the schoolroom last Monday when J went across to open the County Library. One of them was strumming on the piano while the others kept time by cracking their wash-leathers. The librarian's entry, it seems, made a marked difference and there was quite a hush as with assumed severity she took her seat at the high desk. When after a few minutes, however, their leader presented a document to the effect that the windows had been cleaned to the signee's satisfaction, the librarian had to smile as she signed it.

Living as we do between church and inn, school and rickyard, it would be physically impossible to lead the life of a recluse even if we wanted to, which of course we don't. When the pub has a gala night we must, if it is only by bearing with the racket, participate. If, on the other hand, the affair is to the west of us, the early bell calling the faithful in the name of some black-letter saint, we too are awakened and made aware. Neither noise, however, is to be compared with that of the schoolchildren and there again the latest craze is thrust upon us, involving, as often as not, the return of balls,

123

darts, paper aeroplanes, parachutes, etc., which fly over our fence. (Every so often an Upside-Down craze takes the parish by storm, so that glancing out of the window one sees a long row of little girls all upside down and propped by their feet against the school wall. What seems to us strange is that this particular mania affects only the *girls*, who have to tuck skirts into knickers before every such performance, whereas boys would do perfectly well as they were.)

In holiday time the "playground," which is not a playground at all but the church approach and grows a good, feathery, aromatic crop of rayless camomile when given a chance, is used by a handful of young but hardened countrymen who at this season (autumn) make it their solemn duty to copy their elders, and, beginning soon after dawn, till the whole of the large, sloping plot with improvised machinery, up and down, round and round, across and across, in what looks like the most tedious pastime ever invented.

This morning, for instance, one woke to an altercation between two small boys as to which part of the "field" had been harrowed yesterday, which remained to be done to-day. Michael was certain that the lower half had been dealt with, but Leslie was adamant and pressed his case with such conviction that all of a sudden, "Course we never!" exclaimed Michael and the harrowing — performed with a piece of wire fencing coupled to the skeleton of a pushchair drawn backwards by Michael — proceeded, Leslie bringing up the rear with an old bicycle tyre (the baby brother sometimes tows an old piedish) dragged along

124

by a string. (When I saw Michael harnessing himself to the pushchair I began to hope he was a horse. What an old-fashioned notion! It is far more fun roaring away like your father's tractor.)

The farm, with its rickyard on our south-western boundary, is — except for tractors, motor-saws and threshing-machines, dogs, distraught geese, bragging cocks and exultant hens — comparatively quiet; at all events quiet enough for us to miss the arias and folk songs full of the warm south which used not long ago to float in at our bathroom window. The Germans do not sing. They do not, like their Italian predecessors, romp so hilariously with the farmer's baby girl that Roger runs in to ask us, "Why does Pat keep telling them she has wet her nappy and why don't they take any notice?"

One of the prisoners billeted next door now, a cheeky-looking youth with a passion for riding, will sometimes jump on a pony and career round a field or go clattering up the village street. But that is the only sign we see of Teutonic animation. For the rest, they seem hard working and well behaved but glum, as well they may be, sitting in a row on the rickyard wall and, as they stare and jabber together, forming yet another gauntlet for the shy pedestrian to run. (One of our visitors, a girl of eighteen from a remote farm in Shropshire, set out for a walk through our village, but returned at once. The unwinking stares of Sunday Boys *and* Germans had proved too much for her.)

It is particularly unfortunate that the wall they choose to sit on is almost within the shade of our clothes line, for it makes an object they can hardly help staring at and for all a housewife's pride in her wash, there are garments . . . "Well, what would *you* do?" she asked a farmer's daughter in whom she is wont to confide, a competent young woman, never at a loss. "Try hanging them upside down," she promptly advised. "But do you really think that would fool them?" questioned J unconvinced. "Surely they will only think that the quaint English Fraulein wears her knickers a peculiar way?"

One wonders at times what sort of homes these Germans come from, what their background was, how Nazi they were. And there are times when one gets to feeling just a little uneasy about them, as with a child whose punishment may have gone on long enough, however fiendishly it has behaved. A soft feeling this, and one which, had one endured and survived Lidice or Buchenwald, would no doubt have been eradicated. But as a nation we are not good at long-drawn-out punishment, we don't enjoy it, as we are given to understand the Prussian does. When we see glum, worried, anxious faces around us, day after day, month after month, we have misgivings, search hearts and consciences, prod memories — "Remember Lidice, remember Belsen . . ." Yes, but these youngsters here, clean-looking, well-built, frank-eyed, would they have done it? I have seen, scowling hatred from the backs of lorries, types that might; but these . . . ? As one thinks of their families and of the uncertainty of reunion, there comes a doubt; one feels, as I say, just a little uneasy . . .

126

And meantime, what a mixture we are! Oxonians, Londoners, Irish, Germans, three farmers, two motor mechanics, two artists, a dressmaker, a retired woman doctor, a retired baker, a retired butler, rector, postmaster, publican, bicycle man, cow-man, bank manager, airman, journalist . . . What would Miss Mitford have said! (Though it is not so long since, as an aged gardener has assured me, our village was full of beggars, "especially on Sunday"). Few of us live directly by the land. Most are to some extent parasitic, our work, other than voluntary work, having little or no connection with the village itself; which, at any rate in so far as it means changing the character of a place, making it less indigenous and more diffuse, seems a pity.

However, we are still, thank heaven, some way from being a village of week-enders, and one has only to walk a very little way — or indeed just to keep one's door and windows open — to realize that there is any amount of native character left.

This afternoon, for example, found us in the company of a hedger at work beside the footpath that leads down to Hannah's cottage. "Some of it's touchy, we know," he said, indicating the brash, "but that'll burn well, all of it." (Are touchy people inflammable? Or is *noli me tangere* nearer the mark?) "You're welcome to it all," he went on, "there's many as is too lazy to fetch it. They wants you to carry it home for 'em, ah, and sit beside the fire and put it on, some of 'em." There seems no end to his knowledge of woods. For elder he claims the distinction of being the only wood with no poison in it, "that's why they use it for skewers. Vets use it too."

He has, of course, like every countryman who works on his own, with endless time to think, his own decided views about the world at large, wars, politics, weather . . . his last words, called after us as with the shouldered sack we set off up the path, being, "Ah well, us mustn't grumble, us must just keep continuin' on."

To sum up — though I know well I have but touched the fringe of the place — it is as lively a mixed village as you are likely to find, from the white goats on the verge at the south end to the flowery gravel-pits at the north, and from the old orchard with its hedge of sweetbriar (crimson and apricot) on the west to Duke's Wood on the east. And as to our neighbours, for all their different callings, the same strong thread runs through them, binding them together. Whole groups, indeed, are related, so that to be friends with one is to be friends with a family tree, and to be at odds with one might mean offending half the village. (As a neighbour once observed, "It's 'Love me, love my dog, my cat, my chickens, my daughter-in-law, my wife's uncle's cousin and the whole table of kindred and affinity.'")

For better for worse we live at the very heart of it all, returning pilotless planes to schoolboys, running to tell the ex-butler his bees have swarmed (a wonderful system this, involving telephone messages from a distant village), shooing the chickens back into the rickyard, feeding thin dogs, exclaiming at swollen legs . . . There is no end to it, nor to the good turns our neighbours do us and the lively things some of them say. There is gossip, of course, and "loitering and unnecessary conversation" galore; but taken all in all there is good reason why "us mustn't grumble" (why should us?) and every inducement to stay in our village and "keep continuin' on."

(VI) A CARAVAN NEIGHBOUR

Our first introduction was by way of the kitchen window, where she looked in to offer the surprised housewife a chicken.

"Is it a fat one?" J asked.

"Well," said the girl, trying hard to be honest, "it's fatter than it was."

She was not at all put out at our not having the chicken, and when next day, some way out of the village, I caught up with her (she had stopped to tie a lace), she looked up boldly but friendlily and I had the impression that she would not object to my company along the road.

"My name," she said gravely, "is Ellen Marcovitch and I am nine years old." "Do you live in a caravan?" "Yes, better than in a 'ouse; but we're not gypsies, you know. We are Jugo-Slav." "And can you remember your own country?" "Oh no. I was born at London and I like this country, and I don't care if I never see another. I don't go to school because we don't stay long enough, and now I've left them at the hedging because my feet were too cold, but there's only half a chain left to do. I like fruit-picking though . . ."

She prattled on. "Yes, I like towns, but country's better. You see more." "And do you know the birds' names?" "I know them, yes, but I can't tell which they are when I see them." "How about that one," I said, pointing, "you surely know a lark?" "No-no, for me it might have been a tom-tit. I know a magpie though, and I had one once on a Sunday, but on Monday it was gone. My brother it was that catched it and put it in a box, but my Dad got up early to light the fire and he let the bird out." "Why?" "Oh, he didn't want it. You see, we have so much to carry."

We were now rounding the bend that hides the village. "I always like suddenly seeing the stone spire behind that thatch from here," I said. "Yes," agreed Ellen, "and I wonder I would have liked to see them build it and get it so sharp at the top and set that cockerel on it that looks a bit like a bantam. That was before the war, I expect? . . . And is that your little boy I see now, helping his mother in the garden? How old is he?" "Roger's five, and he wants to come and see you and the caravan. How would Sunday do, and perhaps we could all take Sam the spaniel through the wood together?"

She came smelling of wood-smoke, in boots and ragged stockings and an old blue coat with pockets in which she kept her thin brown hands. "I don't like snakes," she said as I opened the wood gate, "I don't like their bodies. Perhaps if I saw one slowly I wouldn't mind, but if you saw one close you could never run fast enough, could you?" "I expect it would be much too scared to chase you," I said, "and anyway they're not as fast as all that; but tell me, do you like the wood?"

130

"I like it, but I thought it would be full of flowers,* violets and those cuckoo flowers. Violets I like best, but I never pick them . . . And how rough and wild it is. It would mean much work cleaning it up, I think?"

We walked on in single file, the path being narrow, till Sam the spaniel who was leading turned off along an even rougher track. "Let's go Sam's way," suggested Roger, and so we did, bending low for the tufted willow, until suddenly Ellen stopped and pointed. "Look at those flames," she said, "is it boys or men?"

I looked across to a patch of dry bracken whence magnificent flames were springing without any apparent check from the Sunday Boys (our village's resident menace) who were beating at them with sticks. As I ran forward they stopped beating and made, as I thought, to bolt; but, "Look at them bobbing down," said Ellen, and sure enough they were trying to hide in the bracken. (Not a bad plan either, if it had been adopted sooner, for two of them were sandy-haired.)

I had recognized them and I let them know it, and the fire now, surprisingly, being out, we went our way. "My brothers are mischievious sometimes," mused Ellen, "one of them likes best to climb trees." "That's what I like," I said, "Does he climb to rooks' nests?" "Oh yes, and we all go nesting, but we don't take eggs. We like to see them. But at Worcester the boys are naughty to birds there. Three or four of them there were and they got pins and found a nest of young birds

* This was early March.

and took out their eyes . . . Those birds wouldn't live, I think?"

As we came out of the wood and trod stubble a lark was singing. "Now don't you know what bird that is singing?" She looked up. "I know it sometimes," she said, and of a sudden she was radiant, a broad smile lighting up her thin face, and laughter wrinkles, looking strangely old for her, playing about the bluish whites of her near-black eyes. "It's the one that flies highest of all, isn't it?" Inevitably I thought of Meredith's "Ascending Lark" — "And every face to watch him raised puts on the light of children praised" — and then she looked down and the spell was broken. "The lark flies as high as an aeroplane, I think? The Spitfire or the Mosskit, is it? I like watching them do the Victory Roll though. We make our dog do the Victory Roll. My brother puts down his face and at once the dog does Victory Roll. We play Traffic Cops with him too. Me and the dog are the cops, you see, and my big brother he is the one that is going too fast, and directly he runs the dog trips him and then I get on top of him and hold him while the dog bites his face . . . But I wish I could speak like Roger," she added irrelevantly. "Oh, but I like the way you speak," I said; and indeed it was charming and so very much her own, with an aitch where she felt like one, a bit of London here and a bit of the country there (for she was no more a Londoner and no less "country" than the average gypsy), and more than a hint of another land in her careful pronunciation of a word like "suffocated" (how she felt "in a 'ouse") and in the introduction of such words as "yet" in unusual places. "I liked the walk in the wood yet," she volunteered as we parted, "and I'd like it in the summer, but I wouldn't like the snakes. I'd be just afraid. You see, those snakes as can't run very fast, they can make *you* run, can't they?"

(VII) A NEW NEIGHBOUR AND AN OLD ONE

It was a pleasant shock this morning to see blue smoke curling up from the chimney of Hannah's cottage. It is months now since Hannah left it; and indeed when we last looked over the empty place we thought it doubtful if a tenant would ever be found with the courage to live in it.

It is a pretty cottage enough, down there beside the stream; roof, walls, all of it of pale grey Cotswold stone, but the roof sags alarmingly and taken altogether, with its ferny well, damp site and lack of space everywhere (especially upstairs), even the toughest and most sanguine countrywoman would feel bound to own that it was in need of much.

However, there was the smoke. She has hoisted her ensign, we thought, this intrepid — or is it desperate? — cottager; and "Look," said J, as we climbed the stile beside the gate and made for the plank bridge, "she must be nice, she has brought wallflowers, and there they are, having a drink in the stream and waiting till she has got things a bit straight indoors and can heel them in."

And so it will be that when we meet this new neighbour, as of course we soon shall, we shall be prejudiced in her favour, for we feel we know and like

133

her already. She is a woman who, in the very thick of trying to make a home out of a hovel, remembers her wallflowers. She is of those who, in Trollope's phrase, "care to do something for the prettinesses of life." We shall show her the wild yellow wallflowers brought as seed from the ruins of Ludlow Castle, for at last, after two and a half years of waiting, we see them flowering on top of our rough stone wall. They are gay and fragrant and hardy and altogether a delight to us, for they remind us of that castle and of the Shropshire Clees, which is always a good thing.

But this morning we passed the cottage and crossed the bridge, and then, instead of turning right as we always used to, for a word with old Bracken, we took the path to the left which leads to the lane and so up the steep little hill to the grey stone village and home.

It is April, and as I sit at the attic window I hear the cuckoo still nest-hunting, although the sun has set behind the rectory chestnuts and the last gleam catches the weathercock on the spire. (The cuckoo is closer now and I can hear its diabolical chuckle.)

Looking down into my neighbour's rickyard I see, in bold lettering across the headboard of a derelict waggon, the name JOHN BRACKEN, and at once memory takes me back to the winter's night when we sloshed through the mud to his farm. Jack the cowman was with me, and so was Jack's young Jim, and since there was no moon we were glad when we came within sight of a glimmer to help keep us to the path.

"Got 'is rushlight, then," said Jack, breaking the silence, "it's a wonder what he does with himself evenings, though, an old chap like that all on 'is own-like, not even a dog . . ."

"But how did he come to this, Jack?" I asked. "They tell me he was once lord of the manor and yet now there's talk of the workhouse."

But Jack "couldn't rightly say." He remembered well enough the man in his heyday, splendidly mounted or smiling a welcome at the manor door; but the decline, it seems, was gradual, so gradual that no one could attribute his ruin to any one cause. At all events, whatever the reason, there the poor old chap was, a man of eighty, under notice to quit and with nowhere to go except the workhouse, with not even a lump of coal for his grate unless one manoeuvred it in a wheelbarrow through the mire. ("Don't trouble yourself again," he had told me, "when this lot's burnt I shall keep to my bed.")

In single file now the three of us follow a rough path through the neglected garden and round to the front of the stone house. To my rap comes a strong "Come in!" and next moment, in the faintly-lit parlour he stands before us, well over six feet, broad, upright, bearded, hands deep in breeches pockets.

"What is it?" he says, head thrown back, bold eyes searching mine.

"You weren't expecting us? We've come for the linen-press, you know."

"It's dark. I expected you sooner."

"I'm sorry. There was milking to see to." (Jack smells strongly of milk.)

"No matter . . . Take it."

The linen-press stands in the darkest corner of the room, invisible save for the great wooden screw outlined against the wall and the play of firelight on the round wooden handles of the only drawer he had used.

(Our cottage, I had tried to explain, was too small for the thing, our staircase too narrow, and in any case the £15 he had been told it was worth was beyond me. But Bracken's mind was made up.)

As we move forward now I feel reluctant to lay hands on it. For all the old man's fierce independence he seems strangely defenceless. I take a quick look round at the few possessions: desk, oilcloth-covered table, tin tray with chipped crockery, grey-sheeted bed, and on a shelf over the black grate three tarnished silver cups . . . "The Philistines be upon thee" keeps running through my head.

But further argument now would only make things worse, and so, having taken the drawers and propped them against an outside wall, we carry the heavy case, like a fat man's coffin, through doors, across wet fields and up the steep hill into the village and home.

By this time young Jim is panting and all three of us are glad of our pints of cider. Then back to fetch the drawers, only to find that they have vanished. "Thought it might rain," explains Bracken, "so I brought them in . . . Sit down, won't you?"

Once again I catch myself wondering what can have happened. And can nothing be done to make him rouse and rescue himself? His orchard, they say, is to be levelled. A tractor will drive in and with chains drag down pear and apple and cherry, hedge and all. Even the magnificent walnut is "too near the house" and so condemned for felling. And yet to all this John Bracken seems resigned, and such is his proud reserve, there can be no reasoning with him.

So we pick up the drawers and thank him and are soon sweating at coaxing and bullying the press up our twisting stairs. Even when, by miracle and brute strength, we have it on the landing, it shies at the entrance to the room where our five-year-old should be sleeping and we have to show it the further flight to the attic.

By now the press has for me become a person, a being impervious to rough usage, averse to corkscrew staircases and small bedrooms and one whose pride prevents him or her from so much as considering an attic. And yet it is at this hopeless moment that inspiration, which comes to smart folk in a flash, plods, as surely as cow to milking, to Jack. I still don't know how he did it. A short groan from the press as the big polished acorn that crowns it is brought low and then there it is standing beside Roger's bed; dwarfing it, true, but decidedly handsome.

"Now that," says Roger, delighted to have company at this hour, "is a thing I should like to sleep with always."

And so there it stands, accepted, distinguished-looking and more useful than we had feared.

At the eleventh hour, when the old farmer had been all but shepherded to the workhouse, from out of the blue popped a distant and quite unexpected relative who, within a day, bundled "grandad," as he called him, off to a remote county and left no address.

An hour after Bracken had gone, Jack's Jim arrived at our cottage with a rather wild-looking parcel, most of it newspaper. "And I was to say," Jim told us, "it was his father's, on his wedding day." "It" turned out to be an exquisitely embroidered white satin waistcoat. But there was also in the parcel a framed sampler completed on September 13th, 1816, by one Emma, "in the ninth year of her age." There are the usual cross-stitch crowns and flowers and tree patterns. There is the alphabet twice over, with one or two carefully stitched mistakes. There are also numbers. But all these of course are merely for getting the hand in. Near the foot of the sampler is a perfectly stitched text —

> With all thy soul love God above
> And as thyself thy neighbour love.

And where is our old neighbour? I wonder each time I look at the sampler and each time I open a drawer of the press. Wherever he is, may he be happy and comfortable and may he never feel in want of a linen-press which, I am strongly convinced, could never be got out of this cottage without major structural alterations. Besides, it has become an ineradicable part of Roger's life.

(VIII) BIRDS

As a boy back at school in a thickly-feathered part of Hertfordshire I was not very surprised to find that of my four hundred odd contemporaries similarly imprisoned only three or four were the least bit interested in birds. For the average child of those comparatively leisured days, the early 1920s, birds were too quick and restless; watching them was altogether too exacting to appeal to any but the crank born with an ornithological bump.

As our own five-year-old — still a little young for the game — has just remarked (telescope to eye), "The proper way is to point the telescope at the sky and look through it and then wait till a bird flies past. Otherwise they're too quick."

That, roughly, was the opinion of most of the schoolboys I used to know. Birds were too quick to be bothered with. But now of course all has been speeded up. If a boy doesn't look very sharp indeed he misses seeing a jet-propelled Meteor altogether. Birds, then, have become, with the exception of a few unhasting insects, the slowest things in the air, while boys, almost *en masse*, have turned into lynx-eyed ornithologists and trained observers.

Not that even now every prep-school lad can be relied on to differentiate between, say, a chiffchaff and a willow-wren. Here, for instance, is an excerpt from an essay by a modern boy of eleven:

"A bird is an animal with two legs. It is not big. The English birds are mostly small. They are very common timmid things, mostly brown with different marks on them. The young birds are always having to be fed. Sometimes they eat each other."

Yet I doubt if Gilbert White's or Richard Jefferies' or even Hudson's first bird note was vivider, and, as I happen to know, the young essayist has since become, in a very short time, a useful naturalist.

Certainly, given the time to look out of our cottage windows, the veriest babe could not help but be to some extent a birdwatcher, were it only to observe the blackbirds at the raspberries and the bullfinches at the peas. Indeed, such were the depredations we were faced with at the last picking, I began to suspect that the huge bill of a hawfinch might have been busy at them. "You don't really think that?" said the gardener delightedly, "why, I'd cheerfully spare a whole row to see a hawfinch." Which, of course, goes for me too . . . *two* rows . . . oh, take the lot.

As for the blackbirds, they are shameless, without even the grace to fly off when we rush out and make savage noises. With a half-wounded, half-blasé air they bob down and scuttle in among the gooseberry bushes so that when we have returned to our interrupted meal they may return to theirs. Of various remedies suggested by more or less helpful friends (we have no netting), the most original has come from the youngest (five): "I know what we'll do. We'll catch the young ones and bring them up the wrong way so as to make them like different sorts of food." His too was the naïve notion for protecting our birds' nests: "Every tree where we know there's a nest we will put a notice on: Do *not* disturb bird."

It is not easy for a child to memorize birds' names, still less their songs. "The ones that say their names, like cuckoo and chiffchaff," he told me, "are easy. The ones I can't remember are ones like thrush and hedgesparrow and linnet." The wood pigeon that calls from the churchyard is, of course, another easy one, with its insistence on "*Two* cows, Roger, take *two* cows, Roger, take *two* cows, Roger, take!" "I haven't *time* to take two cows," Roger, engrossed in building a station, called to it over his shoulder the other day.

And then of course there are birds created expressly for children, or so it would appear from their more or less confiding ways: the robin (for gardeners too and designers of Christmas cards); the sparrow roosting in the plum tree (utility bird with chirp and black bib, two for a farthing); the starling chattering in Nero rhythm from the chimney-pot; the loud wren . . .

Man's presumption never goes further than when he supposes all birds created for himself, for his crops, his eyes, ears and palate and for the entertainment of his young. Yet how convincingly certain birds seem to suit certain people. Where, for example, would the old salt be without his parrot or, for that matter, his old aunt without hers? Or writers to *The Times* without a cuckoo? Or the farmer without his plover or the plough boy without his train of rooks and gulls? Or the superstitious without magpies? Or the Cockney without his sparrows and pigeons? Or the poet without larks and thrushes and nightingales? Not to mention all those intrepid writers and photographers who cheerfully endure fearful hardships on supremely uncomfortable islands in order to earn their cream

141

bowl by reporting on the birds of the sea and the obstinately inscrutable marvel of migration.

With two of the most famous of these I once breakfasted at the house of a third, still more famous. Need I say I kept silent while straining my ears for their lightest word? Here I was at last, in the very home of the Brains Trust. At any moment I might find myself listening to an ornithological discussion of such wisdom, I should do well to remember it all my life . . . I waited. Nobody spoke; until at last the very famous man's charming wife was asked for and gave the recipe for a Swiss kind of porridge; after which we were treated, by the young author of one of our best bird books, to the "Jabberwocky" — in "German." No one would talk shop or mention birds.

Without question there is now no lack of literature on birds by bird-watchers. Some birds indeed — robin, rook, cuckoo and others — have whole books to themselves. What is wanted now is books about men by man-watchers (and about women by woman-watchers), and these of course to be sufficiently unemotional and detached, will need to be written by birds: a contingency which might, at first, seem unlikely if not absolutely out of the question. Yet I myself have seen indications that such volumes — revealing as they are certain to be — may well be on the way and that a rich store of material has in fact already been collected.

In the small round firwood we knew as Goldcrest Wood, in the midst of cornfields, near the Drover's Arms, I remember — could I ever forget? — a goldcrest which flew down from a tree and hovered within a few inches of my nose. For some seconds we stared at each other, eye to eye, the smallest of British birds and a conveniently tall bird-watcher. Certainly I received the impression that that bird was a man-watcher and that, so relatively large and so bland and unwinking was its eye and withal so seemingly intelligent, I had been well and shrewdly observed.

On a more recent occasion, at Blenheim, finding myself on a small lake-island reached by stepping-stones, one of them a flattened kettle, I heard tapping and lifting the binoculars enjoyed a clear and detailed view of that "toned-down king-fisher" the nuthatch, determinedly attacking the upper branches of a dead yew and dropping great slices of bark almost at my feet. I was just thinking how pleasant it was there — the island thronged with cheerful goldfinches and marsh-tits and a great frothing clump of hemp agrimony reflected in the lake, the smell of watermint like an old-fashioned sweetshop — when suddenly there came between me and the nuthatch a round, dark, enquiring eye. The spotted flycatcher was at very close quarters indeed. He was, in fact, perched on a twig a foot or two above me, and staring down sideways into the big black eyes of the binoculars, till my arms ached with holding them still.

On my way home that evening there came vaguely to mind something of Hudson's and sure enough, turning the pages of "Green Mansions," I found him writing of "the clear, brilliant eyes of a bird, which reflect as in a miraculous mirror all the visible world but do not return our look, and seem to see us merely as one of the thousand small details that make up the whole picture."

No doubt he was right; for no man has come nearer to penetrating the bird "mind." On the other hand, it is as well to remember that, short of reincarnation, even the most brilliant naturalist, even the most distinguished scientist, can never crawl within the skin of a living bird and feel as a bird feels, and then crawl out again to tell the tale. He can never quite answer for us that vexed question, upon which so much has been written: Why do birds sing? For even if by some miraculous chance he stumbled on the truth, how could he express it? (No one realized this better than Hudson when he gave Rima a language without words.)

One thing surely is certain, that the songs of birds are not primarily intended for the delight of man. One has only to hear the peacock or listen to the corn-bunting "key-jangling" to realize the width of the chasm dividing man's ideas of melody from birds'. That there is beauty in these harsh bird-noises, such beauty that the sitting hen is cheered through long hours by hearing them again and again and again, is surely undeniable. Indeed, it makes one wonder again about much that is called modern music. Wincing at the discords I feel profoundly sure, as sure as one can be of anything, that this is not beauty, nor in fact music at all. Yet I feel just as sure about the jangle of the corn-bunting than which, to the serenaded hen, nothing, apparently could be more soothing and delightful.

One of the strangest noises I ever heard was a gramophone record of the Lord's Prayer chanted in an Indian dialect; it was laughably grotesque; and yet to those for whom it was intended no doubt it sounded melodious enough, while to them "Hear My Prayer," sung by Ernest Lough, would probably have seemed discordant and meaningless.

Obviously beauty is in the ear of the listener; and when one considers how rapidly science has advanced, so much so that our old-fashioned bodies lag miles behind (they are not up to the strain of the latest jet-propelled aircraft), may it not be that our ears too are outmoded and that many a modern composer has been born hundreds of years in advance of his antiquated audience's appreciation? Alternatively, of course, the time for the appreciation of these noises may have been prehistoric when, as undeveloped creatures with ears hidden among fur or feathers, we were in an early, carefree stage of evolution which we shall never see or hear again.

But that is by the way.

Personally I enjoy listening to birds that tinkle or jingle, like goldfinch and goldcrest, and birds that sing quiet purring songs, like the greenfinch, that go with a drowsy summer afternoon. I like the spring cascades of chaffinch and willow-wren, bubble of curlew, trill of wood-wren, laugh of yaffle, the fountains that fall from lark and tree-pipit, and the casual, desultory notes of the mistle-thrush, like the first heavy drops of rain. Birds that persistently shout and scold and keep on keeping on like a plaguey child (the hysterical type of blackbird, for example) I don't care for so much; but the only bird sound I positively dislike is the thin whine of the robin as, before the end of August, it insists that it is late autumn and that we should be making preparations for heavy snow. Indeed, I have more than once suspected, as it has come squeaking and ticking and whining about our door, doing its utmost to spread despondency, that it is in the pay of the G.P.O., who employ it as a reminder to Post Early for Christmas.

The nightingale I am old-fashioned enough to enjoy, and I shall always be grateful to one in particular which, when a full-sized miracle was called for (I had with me a near-deaf friend who for years had longed to hear it), rose to the occasion and from its hazel twig close beside her poured its song as from a full pitcher into her enraptured ear.

As for the cuckoo, no bird has had more publicity, or should one say notoriety? Shakespeare, you remember, says baldly that it "mocks married men" (a line bowdlerized, believe it or not, into "welcomes the spring!"), and indeed it is readily understandable, though I think regrettable, that the bird has always been considered more or less vaguely impolite. Miss Mitford, for one, couldn't bear it ("My aversion the cuckoo"), and even Delius, who admired it enough to compose a cuckoo tone-poem, made it clear that it was the *first* hearing that moved him, and not, shall we say, the five hundred and first.

Yes, the magic soon goes, but the first hearing is always a delight and a surprise. One forgets from

146

August to April, the slight muting and that what it says is not quite "Cuckoo," but something subtler; not to mention the diabolical chuckle (only heard at close quarters) and the delicious bubbling of the hen, faintly reminiscent of the curlew. All, in fact, that could have been done to avoid monotony in a two-note bird, by making cadence and interval unobtrusive (can you memorize it?) and by making it "laugh" and "stutter," has been done; the bird itself standing out as a creation of supreme wit and genius, a glorious exception, a wonder, a mock-hawk and an extravagant absurdity all in one.

In our village we see plenty of him, but then so we do of a great many birds which like the nearness of wood and farmyard and river. I have known a sparrow-hawk kill a sparrow and drop it within a yard of me in the middle of the village street, and all so swiftly that I only glimpsed the attacker as he sped off towards Duke's Wood, where he was nesting. Later, when high in an old dusty larch (the kind one climbs mainly by faith, heart-in-mouth) I found that hawk's nest, I admired the five eggs and left them alone, though had I been twenty years younger . . .

It was, in fact, a clutch of sparrow-hawk's eggs — excitingly round, bluish-white with great brown blotches — which made me, as a schoolboy, break my vow never to take an egg again. We were on an outing to Wicken Fen at the time, and such was the incentive (the same sort of urge perhaps which made my father spend to his utmost on Tompion clocks), I approached the headmaster — as earnest and solemn a naturalist as

147

ever dissected a daisy — and begged him to sanction my taking one of the four irresistible eggs. Surprisingly he said, "Very well" (perhaps he had the hawk's diet of song birds in mind) and I was up the pine tree and down again with the treasure in my pocket within seconds.

That was the last egg I took. Indeed, I have often preached since, with a fairly clear conscience, against bird-robbery. Even so, it must be said that only those who have been tempted (and I don't mean for cash) can know the all but insuperable strength of this particular temptation. Even now my heart quickens at the sight of blue hedge sparrow's eggs on their bed of bright moss, although I no longer want to take them; and as for Roger, to whom not long ago I gave a warm gull's egg to hold to his cheek (we saw her brooding it again a few minutes later), at five he has already decided that "the egg is the nicest part of the bird."

It is true that, generally speaking, I would rather see the eggs than the newly-hatched young (I was disappointed when in Devon this spring, after many climbs to crows' nests, I at last found the buzzard's I was looking for, and saw, instead of the tawny eggs, three ugly, rabbit-bestrewn young); and yet how infinitely more beautiful than the egg is the full-grown bird, be it gull or goldcrest, hawk or owl.

One winter's day when we were wooding, Roger and I, and a willow log was being climbed for, I looked down into the hollow depths of the tree and saw, shining from the midst of a flurry of tawny feathers, two enormous amber eyes like lamps on a pony trap.

148

My head and shoulders, it seemed, were blocking the doorway of a full-grown tawny owl which now, in a fluttery panic, was rising towards my face. Having firm foothold, I was able to stretch out both hands and catch the owl, which struggled and loudly clipped its bill.

"Why are you being so long?" came Roger's voice from near the foot of the tree. (He, too, had begun to climb.) And then delightedly, seeing my hands full of feathers as I jumped down, "Oh, what is it? Is it alive?"

"Look at its eyes. The trouble's going to be getting us all across this stream."

But somehow the owl, like an obstreperous umbrella, got tucked under my left arm and Roger under my right and the stream was crossed. The owl, I was forced to notice, took advantage of any such ticklish moment (there were two stiles after this) to renew its struggles, while I tried to be firm without hurting it or disarranging feathers which grew to a pattern so flawless that the smallest plume awry must have spoiled it. Indeed, I never saw a neater head, in its dense, wide cap of mottled feathers, and I think we both, owl and I, deplored the November wind as it roughly brushed them the wrong way. At all events, every time this happened the owl showed signs of annoyance, including that very expressive beak-clipping which as clearly as any sound in bird language says "Tut!"

At last we were at our gate, and there was J, oblivious of all but the treasure in hand, planting cuttings from Somerset. I gave a very rough imitation of a tawny owl's call and she looked up into its amber eyes. "How lovely," she said, stroking it. "Try it with a twig," I suggested, "its talons keep reaching for my arteries." But the owl would have none of it, and took a grip of my tweed jacket instead.

Returning *Strix aluco* to its tree was easy enough, though seeing how attentively Roger's every move was being followed by those gig-lamp eyes, I felt a little nervous as to what the talons might do when released. However, I popped it back into the hollow trunk where, rather to my surprise, it stayed, no doubt to preen itself and recover from shock. Roger wanted to "see it at home," but I restrained him. We quite forgot the log of dead willow and, except for a few mushrooms, went home empty-handed.

"I shall remember it all my life," said Roger, and I think he will.

But I must bear in mind the example of that overwhelmingly kind hostess I once heard tell of, and even though this is my pet subject, resist the temptation to go rambling on. To her guest at that time — a famous ornithologist whom she had personally conducted to almost every inch of her large domain — she said:

"And just in case at any time I should not be with you, I must tell you that you may see some birds down that little path there."

(IX) THE RIVER

There is a feeling in our cottage that we are being watched. I don't mean by the village: there the watching is mutual and, thanks to our position, we have the advantage. No, we are constantly watched by dogs: by Paddy the sheepdog, at the kitchen window, and by Sam the spaniel, nose on paws pointed in our direction as he lies in our neighbour's drive, down there beyond the pub, looking towards us soulfully, with that Elizabeth Barrett Browning air of his, as though to will us into taking him for a walk.

This afternoon (Sunday), as I wheeled out my sit-up-and-beg Tourist with Roger already up, Sam saw us at once, and although he must have known it would mean a hot run — for it was that rarity of rarities, a cloudless, shimmering July day — dashed towards us and was soon pounding along, ears flapping, as we free-wheeled through the village and down the slight hill towards the Evenlode. By braking I tried to make the pace more gentle for him, but he only ran on, tongue lolling, ears flying, like an animated bundle of black silks.

"Stop running, Sam!" Roger called to him, "the bike's walking for you, not running. It's walking gently on its wheels."

But in another minute we were at the five-barred gate, and having passed through it and left the Tourist in its usual hiding place, within the double hedge, made our way down beside the barley field, Sam well in front. "Isn't the wheat lovely?" said Roger, "all those oats. Barley, isn't it?"

After the barley we come to the little badger-field, where speculation is indulged in as to what it's like down in the sett and whether the badgers are at home. ("You could tell by sniffing, I expect.")

And now Roger runs on and overtakes Sam. "I'm hotting myself up ready for cooling in the river," he explains, "on the breeze I can smell a lovely fresh smell of the river coming." And in a moment we are there, standing on the little stone bridge with the pool on our right and on our left the weedy bit "like a carpet you could pick up off the river."

Needless to say, Sam is already in. "*Oh*, how I wish I was a dog," sighs Roger, struggling with his shirt buttons, "and could rush straight in instead of having to stop and take off clothes. There's only Sam's collar to get wet and he doesn't mind that." Sam's fur is decidedly serviceable, and how nobly he treads the water; it is his serious business, this swimming, a thing he has to do and do well, head up, the water rippling away from the shining black curls of his back. Oh, well swum, sir! But for pity's sake keep away from our clothes and don't shake that great sopping hearthrug all over them.

We are both in now, at a little distance from the deep pool, and both up to our necks, for it is an accommodating stream, this, with levels for all sizes and ages. It is icy but glorious and the smell of water-mint and codlins (willow-herb) better than bath-salts. In the distance a train chuffs fussily towards London. "Suppose we were in it?" gloats Roger, "still, I don't mind a train journey if there's a river at the end of it or a bit of sea."

"I'm going down to Mummy's bathing-place," I call out, "come and see if you're brave enough for it," and together we paddle through the shallows till we reach the narrow channel where the river takes a plunge into what used to be a clear, natural bath. (Here it was that, last summer, to Roger's ecstatic delight, four village boys played ring-a-ring-o'-roses, all submerging completely at "we all fall down"). Now, however, the watercress, in two waves of glossy green, has swept in on it, leaving only a foot or two's breadth of water free. After some hesitation Roger lets himself be lifted in, while the minnows bump inquisitive noses against my ankles. But it is really too deep for him, and having yelled to be helped out he tries to hide among the watercress and then suggests we do some "real swimming" back in our usual place.

It is not, for his part, swimming at all, but as I tow him round on his back he seems to be getting the feeling, which is about as much, I suppose, as can reasonably be expected of a child of five. At all events he loves going in and we don't mean to put him against it by rushing him.

As children go, he is obedient, but it is never easy getting him out of a river, and now, no sooner is he out than he rushes back again. "Goes right in like a little old duck, don't 'e?" says a voice, "don't 'e look little in there, though?" It is a small ragged boy with his brother, from a nearby cottage, both armed with rods (of a sort) and jam-jars. Roger is charmed with his audience and decides to stay in indefinitely. There is a good deal of splashing and laughter, which all goes with the river and the day.

"You won't 'arf cop out, though, if old Donovan sees you in there!" says one of them. "Is it true that he has

153

tried to stop people bathing here?" I ask, "tell me what happened." (I know very well, from our excellent bush-telegraph, but I want their version.) In a few jerky phrases he tells me how the farmer, returning from a fuel-fetching expedition to his hayfield beside the river, found all his men and boys (dark Oxfordshire) together with the sunburnt German prisoners (husky blonds) in the river, their ugliness — ragged jackets and caps and P.o.W. shirts and trousers — abandoned and piled with rakes and pitchforks "in most admired disorder" upon the bank. Whereupon the bathers were ordered out, and in forceful terms of the plainest possible Irish a comprehensive veto was thundered forth. "'e can't stop me, though," the waif added menacingly, "give 'im a box o' the ear-'ole, I will." I noticed, however, that neither he nor his brother bathed.

As I dragged Roger out and dried him I thought of the former owner of those riverside meadows who, according to the wise man of the village, used to "work and sweat and jump in fifty times a day and shout, 'Come on in, boys, and have a ride on my back!'" O fortunatus nimium . . .

At this point the two urchins betook themselves and their tackle to fish the pool by the bridge, while Roger launched his toy boat and I produced a large plantain leaf for its sail. Such an adjunct, however, would only mean "more unneeded work," I was told, and I was asked to find a "strong, suitable, stick-like reed" for a mast instead.

At the fourth attempt I found the acceptable and in the meantime I had collected a handful of flat stones for Ducks and Drakes; for though I cannot call myself a fisherman (directly my bait goes in it is flocked to as manna by what Milton calls a "finny drove" of extremely small fish which swarm upon it and chase it all over the pool until it has been devoured), I will challenge all comers to a fairly-umpired contest at Ducks and Drakes: all, that is, save a certain schoolboy who has devoted an untold number of hours to practise. He it was who taught me the rules of the game, or rather, its language. You knew, I expect, that when your stone hops once it's "ducks" and that when it hops twice it's "drakes", but there is much more to it than that. When it hops three times it's "geese," four times "ganders," five "swans," and so on to "turkeys" and "turkey-cocks," "turkey-cocks" standing for no fewer than fifteen bounces. I supposed that after "turkey-cocks" must come "herons" and "dodos," but my informant, who likes to throw downstream and against the wind, told me he had never got further than "turkey-cocks" himself.

And so the afternoon wore on, while Sam hunted among the teazles and willow-herb, all netted in goosegrass, and put up a scolding sedge-warbler; and a cock reed-bunting charmed its mate (not us) with its persistent "Hip, hip, hip," which is the nearest it ever gets to cheering; for all its dawn-to-dusk efforts to shout "Hooray!" Small dragonflies rested on reeds and grasses as though to give them flowers, dark blue, steel blue, and that glinting copper that is neither brown, green nor gold, but something of each. Bees visited the loosestrife, peacock butterflies probed the teazles . . .

155

Suddenly — it is always suddenly — a kingfisher sped by, making us both exclaim: "It's been fishing for kings," said Roger, "the king of the fishes."

Then, tiring of boaties, we wandered over to the bridge, where the boys had fished and potted quite a haul of minnows. "Those things don't keep for long, do 'em?" said the one that did the talking, throwing a dead minnow back into the pool, "ah, but I had one that long the other day," he said excitedly, at the same time putting a very respectable distance between grubby, held-up palms. "And it got away?" "That 'e didn't," he said stoutly, "not with me be'ind 'im."

So we sat on the bridge for a while and watched the water, while the urchins caught more mites and talked of monsters. There was talk of ants too, "emmetts" as they called them (so did Milton): "There was flyin' emmetts on this bridge, thousands on 'em. We took and drownded 'em." And while they chattered on I kept watching the river and thinking of where, some fourteen miles up, we had known it before.

It was at Foxholes, near Bruern Abbey and just below Bould Wood, that I first came to know and feel the Evenlode, and I took it as a good omen for our further friendship that when I first bathed there, just there where a wide bend makes a willow-hung pool well stippled with yellow nenuphars and the bluest of river forget-me-nots, I found a magnificent plant of the pink-crowned flowering rush.

Later we were to know that little promontory intimately, and at all hours: at dusk, when an otter, intent on a short cut across the grass, heaved itself

156

dripping from the pool and ran behind us, to slip into the river again without a ripple; and by moonlight too when, after a sweltering summer's day, the black water felt warmer than the night air.

It is this same river which takes the flow from that mysterious chain of lakes in the heart of Wychwood Forest, a chain ending, as I remember it, in a most secret round pond walled in by trees and reflecting a swan upon her nest. It is the same those Romanized Britons dwelt beside at North Leigh, the same Warde Fowler* wrote of at Kingham, and the same that, near Bladon, receives the exhausted Glyme after its fantastic adventures at Blenheim, before flowing on to join the Thames at last below Wytham Great Wood, about five miles (as the Thames flows) from Oxford . . .

I look up now to see J walking down the badger-field to meet us. "Who *were* those boys?" I ask when we are out of earshot. (I never can remember, as she does, who everybody is.) They are part, I am told, of a family of eleven and "have to work like men, that's why they look so disillusioned and ragged and tufty . . . Was it cold in the river?"

Roger admits that it was but that he was "just brave enough to hide in a bed of watercress," where a horsefly bit him. "I usually manage to swipe them before they do any damage," I put in, "but you're still a bit young to overtake them." He protests that he

---

* Historian, naturalist, don, author of very readable bird-books. Discovered marsh-warblers nesting in Kingham osiers when the bird as a British nester was practically unknown.

"overtook three," and adds irrelevantly, "I shall call this a *short* day. The minute we were out of church it was in to dinner. The minute we were down at the river it was back to tea. It's wonderful, really, how we manage to use the short time we have at all."

Nothing, it's true, goes more quickly than a river day — a real old-fashioned scorcher when "the wind's never noth'n more than jist light air" — and yet even in winter, when the teazles are black and the wind's a skinner, it's good to walk beside "our" river, smelling and hearing it and playing Ducks and Drakes and anything else you can think of to keep you warm. With the slightest encouragement, the weakest of March suns, or even without it, we begin to think of bathing, peering down through the muddy turbulence to catch a glimpse of our bathing-place — our summer place of pebbles and watermint and clear water and of those three so nicely graduated depths — and hoping with the high hope of spring and childhood that, as Roger puts it, it will "come to the surface again soon."

(X) ANGLO-ROMAN INTERLUDE

I gave her a shilling and opening the slim book she handed me read, "Visitors are advised to ask at the cottage for two keys and a candle."

It seemed a promising start. True, the effect was a little spoiled by our being offered an electric torch instead of a candle; but where the imagination is at full stretch — and if a jumble of stones is to be conjured into walls and colonnades, it must be so here — torch becomes candle with but a very slight effort.

"I suppose coins and things are still being found?" I suggested.

"Not that I've heard tell of," said the caretaker, "but there, the Germans have just been at it, and what they found nobody knows."

One would have liked a word with those Germans, I thought, as we took a narrow path between grass-filled "rooms" and not so much as to their finds as to their feelings on being compelled to clear the site of a Roman villa, at five bob a week. In their absence, the "German Prisoners of War Forever!" they had chalked on the shed protecting the mosaic gave one no notion of a would-be invader's attitude towards those who had acted on the same idea and with more success.

As at Chedworth (20 miles due west along Akeman Street), one stands amazed at the wall-heating system in what the guidebook calls the best winter room. (Key number one.) Indeed, it is the residents' determination, in the face of mists from the neighbouring Evenlode, to keep warm, and their ingenuity with hollow bricks, which endear them to us far more than the pains they took with the geometric designs of their tesselated floors.

And who were they? It was a surprise to me to learn that they were probably not Romans at all, but "Romanized Britons and men of peace, possibly members of a British nobility owning their own estates, possibly men who had acquired wealth. The pleasant valley close to Wychwood," the guide-book goes on, "must always have been attractive, especially to the

Briton who was a keen huntsman, then as now . . . British hunting dogs were almost as celebrated in Rome as were British oysters."*

Certainly it is more flattering to envisage one's ancestors well mounted and in the equivalent of hunting pink, or alternatively, in warmed rooms and decorous togas, toying with their oysters, than, as one had rather feared, prancing about in woad and cocking snooks at the pampered invader.

Four of their oyster-shells, which Roger found among loose tesseræ and dabbled in the river, might from their whiteness have been emptied but yesterday at the Savoy. But we came across no oyster-openers, as did the excavators at Chedworth, nor bangles of worked bronze, nor even coins. All things considered, it looks as though, compared with the great villa at Chedworth — happened on, you remember, by a rabbiting party which had lost its ferret — this at North Leigh, for all its three quarters-of-an-acre of courtyard, was a mere cottage with, for the servants, "poorish rooms and small bath."

The head on the earliest coin found at Chedworth is that of Domitia, wife of Domitian, A.D. 81-96; but there are much later coins too. Someone in Charles II's reign was careless enough to leave a farthing; and someone else with a hole in his pocket in the time of Edward VI must have found himself the poorer, on reaching home, by a silver penny.

* "The Roman Villa at North Leigh, Oxon," by M. V. Taylor (O.U.P.).

If comparable riches lie buried at North Leigh (and much excavating still remains to be done), only the rabbits know of them. All that can be seen now is low walls and mosaic and harebells and a few Roman snails (roasted brandyball colour in the burning of the scrub), and a lead pipe which was the waste of the plunge-bath now enclosed in a semi-subterranean washhouse. It was for this last that we had been lent the torch and key number two.

We glanced at the ancient bath and admired the modern washhouse, which boasted among other things a scrubbed brick floor and a copper, a bundle of billhooks and sickles, two bow-saws and a scythe. "I could do with a place like this," we both said at once. Returning to ground level we found ourselves beside the caretaker's potato patch . . .

Yes, to return to Roman times would mean going without potatoes, though on the other hand there would be none to insinuate themselves into the flour. And then the hot baths, the warm rooms, the oysters . . . Ah, but what if one were not "of the British nobility" nor even of those who had "acquired wealth"? What if one were consigned to the servants' quarters, with a poorish room and a small bath to share with the other slaves?

And even if one could be sure of the blue blood and the denarii, would not the inevitable decline and fall of the villa, due to "ruthless imperial taxation and corrupt officialdom," give one pause? For "little by little," as the North Leigh chronicler gloomily records, "the economic organization of Britain broke down and

161

wealth dwindled. Owners of large estates must have found it more and more difficult to maintain them. Finally the Saxon, breaking through all defences, penetrated up the Thames Valley . . . The new lords, unaccustomed to such houses, did not rebuild, but took up their abode elsewhere, leaving the Roman house to fall into ruins and become a quarry, until in course of time its walls were levelled and the grass grew over them . . ."

A dismal finish, and one is still left to wonder so much. At what stage, for instance, did they give up their oysters or did they cling to them as indispensable till the very last? Did they rail against Caesar and his tax-gatherers or did they go down sheepishly and without a murmur, adopting the same sort of philosophy as that of our Oxfordshire hedger who said, "Us mustn't grumble. Us must just keep continuin' on?" I wonder.

CHAPTER
FOUR

Glyme* Influence

(1) THE DUKE'S PHEASANTS

In every thriving village one still finds at least one man who can turn a capable hand to anything, Jack-of-all-trades and master of the lot, and with his own particular craft — carpentering, it may be, or smithing or its modern equivalent (mending bicycles and such) — thrown in.

Certainly we are lucky to have Frank Mason in our village. His workshop is indeed the very hub of it, rivalling The Stook & Sickle as clubroom or centre of news and entertainment; while our own possessions — bicycles, lawnmower, alarm-clock, mincer, mechanical toys — join in a multi-voiced hymn of praise, not merely to his ability but to the *nil desperandum* spirit in which he handles a tired piece of mechanism which almost anyone else would turn down as hopelessly past repair.

* The Glyme is a small river which, rising in the Heythrop neighbourhood, near Chipping Norton, is joined by the river Dorn near Wootton and continuing southward by way of Woodstock attains its full glory [*sic*] at Blenheim, where Capability Brown widened it into a lake before sending it down Cascades to join the Evenlode.

No neighbour knows more about our old cottage than he does, for he used to live in it before he moved to his neat little place down the street, and I seldom leave his shed without something mended and something learnt too about Church Cottage's history.

"I minds the time," he began this evening (a most promising opening) "when there was more pheasants hangin' in your house than in any other house in the village. There was a man livin' there, see, as'd buy all the lads could shoot, down there in Duke's Wood, and take 'em to market, ah, and there was always a steady supply for him to pay cash for too. Three o'clock in the mornin' you'd hear 'em down there, lads and boy-chaps y'know, unemployed they all were (you don't see the likes o' them now) and nothin' better to do than be down the wood nights, when there was a moon, ah, and often in broad daylight too. Keepers and police'd come enquirin' through the village 'times, but I can't say as I ever saw anyone go back along with 'em."

Church Cottage is never hung with pheasants now (would that it were), though Sam the spaniel will sometimes put one up from the bracken and startle us all (himself included) as with a cry like a klaxon the cock beats its way out to blunder through the trees, its barred tail quivering like a thrown knife.

Our salvation, it seems (I mean our freedom of Duke's Wood), lies partly in His Grace's beneficence, which is truly bountiful and extends far beyond the nine-mile-long wall at Blenheim, partly in the fact that there is no grain ration for the pheasants, which otherwise might be thought to need the wood to themselves.

It would indeed be a blow to us if ever the wood were closed, for as it is we can say with Comus that we

> know each lane and every alley green,
> dingle or bushy dell of that wild wood;
> and every bosky bourn from side to side
> our daily walks and ancient neighbourhood.

Yes, even though Comus or a spirit much like him inhabits it, playing tricks upon the stranger and making him crawl through blackthorn on hands and knees . . .

But first let us look at the wood from its station (not its village) side, from down there by the white stile which leads from the road into the station footpath. The path, bordered with knapweed, runs between cornfields to the wood and through a part of it to the buttercup field below the village which, from that stile, appears to be planted in the very middle of the wood, the spire a tree — a stone pine, perhaps, or a wellingtonia — taller and more formalized than the rest, with young ash and a few high larches and sycamores frothing round it and the weathercock, veiled it may be in blue incense from cottage chimneys, perched triumphantly on its topmost twig.

It is the spire which Comus relies on to mislead the unwary, even as wreckers used to count on their treacherous lights. Not that the spire is normally anything but a reliable landmark, to be looked to now, from miles off, as surely as it was by pious pilgrims hundreds of years ago.

It is simply that in Duke's Wood there is a path, a primrose path indeed, straight and broad, which, having just left the shade of the firs (they make a wood within a wood and in the midst of it) you look along joyfully; and when you see that it leads straight to your trusty landmark the church spire, you take it gladly, blessing your guardian angel and stepping out in high hopes of being, for once, in very good time for luncheon.

At this point Comus sniggers, but you ignore the cackle, which sounds like a magpie's, and go striding on until . . . until you come to the blackthorn, the merest spinney as it seems at first, with the spire just beyond; and then, as you try to shove your way through it, it quickly becomes a thicket and a thicket of such fiendish impenetrability that, as I have said, you are forced to your knees to make any sort of headway at all. You may think that I exaggerate. If so, I can only invite you to try for yourself, for I am by no means the only one on whom Comus has played his joke; but I shall not come with you. I like to walk in the wood. Crawling, with inch-long thorns exploring hands and knees, has little attraction.

So much for what we know as the path that isn't a path. The true paths through the wood, the ones we use oftenest, are First Path and Second Path, each having its well-defined track and character, each its own individual assortment of flowers and trees. First Path is the one for hazel-nuts and for stooping the whole length of it, in summer and autumn, till you come to what we call the Imitation Fir Wood (to distinguish it from the Real Fir Wood. It is an old copse containing a handful of larches and spruces).

Opposite that copse is the best patch for spring flowers, and it was there that Roger, in the company of two other boys, was once asked if he knew the colour of bluebells (the questioner was a colonel with a weakness for riddles), and was told no when he suggested "blue." "And so what colour did he say they were?" we asked. "Oh, we ran away quickly," said Roger, "before he could tell us."

At the Imitation Fir Wood we may stop and build a "house" or go in for serious wooding; but usually we turn right along the autumn-crocus track to Second Path which, except at high summer when it is blocked by a tangle of yellow melilot, is wide and clear, leads home and has wide cart tracks at either side of it.

Only once have we seen a cart there and that was in early April when the Duke's men had come for their annual cutting of pea and beansticks. We spoke with them of dukes and pheasants and vegetable-growing and admired the neat bundles of ash and hazel and the new spaciousness which their chopping had made at the craneshill corner of Second Path. "We thought that the marks were olden-day marks," said Roger afterwards, looking at the cart tracks, "but they still belong to the woodmen."

Duke's Wood is not a wood of huge old trees but rather of plantations — ash, fir, hazel — with more or less dense undergrowth of blackthorn, bracken and brambles. The few big trees there are don't seem to flourish and in the Imitation Fir Wood there is more

167

than one dead wych-elm stretching up gaunt, bare branches among the firs and cracking ominously at every breeze.

From time to time one attacks their lower branches, but it takes two men with a cross-cut saw, or a full gale, to bring one down; and it was after a night of tempest last winter that we came upon the wreck of one of these giants, with a Commando and an Air Force man standing, like axe-armed pigmies, beside it. The storm had cracked the trunk almost through, about fifteen feet up, so that the tree had toppled without falling, its upper branches entangled in neighbouring trees, while other branches had showered down, making what looked like heaps of long, dry bones filmed with green powder, and these kept us in kindling for many weeks.

At the moment when we first saw them the two amateur woodsmen were planning the attack and, even as we watched, the Commando (a smallish man made entirely of muscle) ran up the steeply-leaning tree and, standing upon the shattered ledge where the tree had broken, rained blow upon blow with an enormous axe at the narrow strip of wood still holding the two sections of the trunk together. It looked appallingly risky, and each time the tree cracked, which it did often, we held our breaths, while from Sam, half buried in a rabbit-hole, came muffled yelps which seemed to mean that he too was anxious.

The strength in an inch or two of wood, even dead wood, always seems to me remarkable. Some tons of wych-elm, lightly held above, hung now by what appeared to be rotten bark and continued so to hang, for all the Commando's strength and effort. (At times we could see no more than the back of his khaki trousers which, withstanding the fullest possible tension, said much for the thread and the stitching in battle-dress.) In the meantime his mate had thrown up one end of a hastily fetched wireless aerial with which the Commando, at the fifth attempt, lassoed one of the thicker branches. Chopping ceased while the three of us heaved and strained at the aerial, and, when it snapped, fell in a heap, leaving the tree still standing.

Chopping was then resumed, accompanied by sickening and even more frequent cracks, until suddenly the whole tree, except for the bottom fifteen feet, leapt into the air and landed with the noise of a thunderclap to plant itself deeply, close beside the original base, its branches still held by another wych-elm and a spruce.

And where was the Commando? At the critical moment he had, like a squirrel, taken a flying leap and landing clear of the tree rolled over and over in the ivy till he came to our feet. He then stopped rolling, picked himself up, grinned and strolled over to see exactly what his axe had done. Any ordinary man would at least have sprained a wrist or an ankle. Not so he who, from his yellow hair, J has nicknamed Bobby Shaftoe. These Commandos are tough.

Spectacular as it all was, "a fine and thrilling operation" (see *Our Village*), turning Roger pink with excitement, it took me several hours, on later, solitary visits, to complete the felling. For no sooner had I climbed the neighbouring wych-elm and with bow-saw

169

freed the dead tree from that than it crashed down on to a small oak tree, where precariously perched in the crown, I found it supported again by an astonishingly thin twig. When it finally crashed it made the noise of a small bomb and set going the klaxons of every pheasant in the wood.

It was surprising how quickly all that beautiful, dry timber disappeared. Our extravagant fire burned much of it, fiercely, with an almost white flame; but I made no effort to compete with the tireless Shaftoe who staggered up the buttercup field again and again with such burdens as made the back ache to watch him and reminded one of those ants which "undertake gigantic loads for honour's sake." I even offered to help, but he shook his head. "You'll find a heap of stuff ready chopped back there," he said, indicating the wood, "take as much as you like." As it happens, I enjoy hewing my own, but — well, that's how they are in our village.

In summer, when the iron basket in our fireplace carries the same unburnt logs day after day and we no longer feel guilty at returning from a walk without a "shoulderpiece" or at least some dry twigs, we go down to the wood purely for pleasure and to indulge children and dogs in their various more or less innocuous sports and games. Sam will lead us if he can to a certain waterhole — little more than a deep puddle, where a spring has bubbled up beside a rose bush in one of the more secluded parts — there with dignity to submerge and turn his coat of black curls into a bathing suit, and shake it happily all over us if he gets the chance. After which he may dig in the sunny place we call our own

(J discovered it), where the turf is kept like a lawn by the rabbits, and small conifers planted at wide intervals offer just the right amount of shade. To Sam's dismay, Roger likes to "help" with his digging and even enjoys the feeling of blunt claws scratching at his shoes when the spaniel tries to get the hole to himself.

Our wood games are not very original — Savages, Pirates (a thunderstorm adds realism), Keepers, the latter entailing the prompt production of a permit from the Duke himself. Having no such permit, one is obliged to improvise; three hazel-nuts, for instance, giving one a bare three minutes in which to leave the wood. When it came to my turn to be keeper, this afternoon, Roger could produce nothing more convincing than a dock leaf, which I reckoned might last him about half an hour, there being just that time left before tea. "But I want to camp in the wood and stay here for ever," he protested. I could only refer him to the supreme authority who, in His Grace's absence, happens to be Sam, and although he refused to be diverted from his rabbit hunt Roger made him answer in a gruff but affable, dog-of-the-world sort of voice, "Why of course, if you come from a far country and your wife is horrible, of course you may stay as long as you like." This was a new turn (wives don't usually come into a game of Keepers), and I asked what sort of thing a horrible wife might be expected to do. "Oh, find you a job just as you wanted to go for a walk, that sort of thing," he said.

At other times we may go tree climbing, for the fun of it, or to look into a nest or throw down those long fir cones — Roger's favourite thing is exploring, "finding a new climbing tree and a new little path" — but on most wood walks one likes to be quiet, seeing flowers and trees, listening to birds. So far, with the feeling always of rarity-round-the-corner, we have seen nothing less common than the crimson grass-vetchling (and it *is* uncommon in these parts), which J found there this summer, and the autumn crocus. Of orchises, broad-leaved Helleborine grows strongly, a single stem beside Second Path bearing forty fine, starry, mauve-green flowers, while one of the many plants of the early purple has produced a tall spike with every flower pure white, as pretty a thing as any in the wood and as dainty as its honey-sweet cousin the butterfly.

The commonest flowers of Duke's Wood are melilot, woodspurge, St. John's wort, dog's mercury, nettled-leaved bellflower, bluebell, primrose and teazle, the latter a great collector of rain which it stores charmingly in deep green cups between prickly stem and leaves. They are the kind of thing, like shepherd's purses (which we used to break open to see if they contained gold or green copper) one remembers most vividly from childhood. As soon as he could toddle Roger was fascinated by them, collecting oddments for a sponge and then dipping it in to wash his "stiff" (sticky) face.

Perhaps because the wood lacks old oaks and dense clumps of nettles we seldom hear the nightingale there. Once, however, when the three of us had spread a rug on the lawn near Sam's water-hole, an obliging bird began singing from a rose bush just above us. "Listen!"

I told Roger, who had already started combined operations with Sam, "it's the nightingale." He stopped digging for a minute, and then, "D'you mean that tweety noise?" he said.

For myself I like always the stroll up the buttercup field, from wood to village, as well as the wood itself, with a fine sloe-and-field-rose hedge (beloved of long-tailed tits and bullfinches) beside us and ahead the spire and the village, with blue smoke curling up among its many walnuts and chestnuts. The field itself is studded with molehills (oontie-tumps, as Scots call them), making lumpy beds for cows. "Isn't it funny," Roger was saying as we passed them, "how much commoner cows are than bulls? You see any amount of cows but so few bulls. You would have thought all those cows would have husbands, but they don't, not judging by how little you see of bulls."

As we climb the stile into the village we can see how old Jeremiah's vegetable patch is doing and compare the progress of his rows with ours. "My peas are up too," J told him one spring day. "Be 'em?" he snapped, surprised, and, I think, displeased. "He meant 'Be *them*,'" said Roger.

(Which reminds me of another old gardener-neighbour whom we watched sowing parsnips, close beside a path frequented by schoolchildren. "They don't fancy 'em," he explained, "they'll pull a carrot but they won't touch parsnips. Peas, though, ah, peas, they'll lie down to they.")

And now we are back in the village, Sam going to his home and we making for ours, treading on the camomile to loose its apple fragrance, Roger running ahead to open the green gate. I dump my log and go up to the attic to finish a chapter and as always glance up at the weathercock before I begin. In our absence it has swung right round to point due east — towards Church Cottage and Blenheim Palace and (lying between the two) Duke's Wood.

Yes, there is much to be said for living on a hill by a river and still more if your hill is near a wood. Long live the Duke, then, and Heaven alone preserve his pheasants, living out their quiet lives under the bracken, with nothing more deadly than an occasional, rather slow spaniel to disturb them. Meantime let Providence be blessed for giving us trees and grassy paths as our close neighbours, and as a not very distant one a duke so well disposed that, without even one TRESPASS notice to deter us, he lets us wander at will along First Path and Second Path and among the firs and, in fact, throughout all the tangled length and breadth of that wholly delightful playground known to us as Duke's Wood.

(II) BLENHEIM FIFTY YEARS AGO

It was late one winter's evening when our neighbour and friend Johnny (*né* Gerald) Horne came along to our cottage with a jar of honey (he keeps eighteen hives) and began to reminisce. It was very late indeed — for I had egged him on — when he left, and I was saying to J how I wished I'd had a notebook by me.

When I did take a notebook to his house I was prepared for it to kill his breezy talk at birth, but with his usual unrufflable air Johnny began his tale of Blenheim and when I came to transcribe it I rejoiced to find how strongly his personality had come through.

Imagine then the three of us sitting beside an old kitchen range, a range bright with metal polish and black lead and the red-hot coals glowing behind the bars. Mrs. Horne (Nellie) sits opposite me, the kind of comfortable woman you know at a glance can be relied on from the first black olive to the last ratafia biscuit. She has large, lustrous eyes. Indeed, as Horne himself says, "she is really lovely." Drake, a black retriever, has a paw on my shoe and keeps nudging me to stroke him, which of course makes shorthand writing difficult. On my right sits Johnny Horne. He has insisted on my taking his upholstered, fireside chair while he sits upright on a wooden one. He is sixty-two and so like the old family retainer of film and fiction that any Hollywood director would sign him up on sight. The only visible divergence from type is in his expression which far from being wooden gives you the idea that he has just enjoyed a good joke and is about to enjoy another.

He has not only a long memory but an orderly one, so that his story unfolds smoothly and chronologically, with only a very occasional reminder from Nellie.

As for the spacious times he tells of — the banquets, the black page-boys, the special trains — however fervently we may condemn them and be thankful that the abuses that sometimes went with them are not part of our more realistic age, we cannot most of us fail to enjoy vicariously the fun these grand people *and their*

175

servants had. We read of the royal banquet at Blenheim and the torchlight procession crossing the lake, or we stand before Tissot's picnic with its Nankeen teapot and Vichy bottles and fur rugs and tell ourselves — we who have spent all our lives, it may be, at Brixton or Penge West — that we too have lived in Arcadia.

Mind you, if you happened to be a footman it was tiresome to have to keep powdering your hair, or if a kitchenmaid and in love it was galling not to be able to wear your engagement ring for all to see; but to set against those little bothers you could at least be sure of the best possible food and drink, and if your "place" was a good one, a great many cheering treats and concessions besides.

Need I add that Johnny ultimately became a London butler and that he and his housekeeper-wife were given "full charge of everything, including the engagement and pay of sixteen servants"? The sixteenth, by the way, was a boy who, when sent on errands, would absent himself for several hours, returning at last with the excuse that he had "been to Buckingham Palace, sir, to see the King and Queen." "I thought at first he must be trying to pull my leg," the ex-butler told me, "but no: he was so patriotic he used to go and stand there for hours. Once in a while he did catch sight of them and on those days we had to rely on someone else."

But Johnny's stories — blithe times at Long Leat, his sea days with the admiral and so on — are legion, and I hope one day to give him a book to himself.

At forty-five he retired and to-day one has only to see his large, orderly garden and taste its produce to know something of how usefully he has spent these possibly less arduous years.

When Horne saw the Blenheim part of his story made the feature article of *Country Life*, he was of course pleased. But for sheer unrestrained delight I turned to Nellie, and I was not disappointed. It was she who had unearthed the engaging photograph of Horne as a hall boy, and when she heard that it was in *Country Life* she took it from me with a cry of "Where's my Johnny? Let me see my Johnny!" kissed it and hugged the magazine to her admirable bosom. It was all most heartening . . .

But here's Johnny at my elbow. Let him speak for himself.

On the Blenheim Estate

During the whole of my parents' married life of forty-five years neither had a holiday. They just seemed to live for the family and to do everything they could to make life sweet for us. Mother made all our clothes. I was the youngest, and as Father and four brothers had to wear them before they came to me, there was not much left to hold me together. In common with most of her neighbours, Mother did a good deal of gloving. Every Saturday I took the gloves she had made into Woodstock, and for this and other odd jobs she would give me a ha'penny. With a ha'penny, in those lean days, I can tell you I felt marvellously well off; and I can tell you I earned that ha'penny too. The way from our place to Woodstock lay through Blenheim park, and I used to dread taking it on account of the deer. Oh, but they were a lot of dangerous swines — and how they bellowed when they were rutting! I didn't know what to do, go on or turn back, but I kep' on and just got by. They put up notices, d' y' see, BEWARE OF THE RED DEER, so that you never got nothink, not even if the old things killed you.*

At harvest time, day after day Mother packed a meal and took us into the harvest field to help lease the corn. It was a nice healthy custom and I enjoyed it, the only snag being the harvest bug, a shocking thing which simply irritates you to death. I remember a sack of excellent flour from the corn we had leased. All the corn was hand-cut with a sickle, a man and his family undertaking to reap and bind so many acres on their own; very much as it must have been in the days of Ruth.

As for schooling, I played truant as a regular thing, swarming up the inside of an old oak and sitting in a most unhappy position among the branches until the others came out. Then I'd climb down and march home with them and no one the wiser. You would think I'd be missed, but the truth was in those days people went in for such large families, the school was packed and nobody noticed or bothered much if one little boy wasn't there. And home lessons — well, I just refused to do them and got the cane in consequence

* The first Woodstock gloves are said to have been made from hides from the park deer.

every morning I went to school; while during the day, as likely as not I'd be caned again for playing about. We were caned always on the hand — never "trouser-ointment" — though if that didn't make us cry (and me it never did), back and legs might get it too as we ran away.

The only thing I shone at was map drawing; all my other work was rather bad. When I first started I had to take a copper or two to pay for my education, but free schooling soon came in and put a stop to it. We had a splendid schoolmaster, overworked of course. He was a very successful bee-keeper and I think the hives that do so well for us now owe much to his example. The other day I went to see him and do you know what he said? "Gerald," he said, "you were one of my best pupils. I shall never forget you. You never gave me a bit of trouble." And this to a "boy" who can't remember one school day without the cane!

A good deal of our free time, as boys, was spent playing on the railway — putting pins on the line and other such mischief — or down at the river fishing. In those days fishing in the Evenlode was free and no one questioned our right there, but as time went on the Duke made everyone take tickets, which were five shillings each for the season, and then you could fish whenever you liked. But five shillings was of course beyond us, and beyond most of the villagers.

My first earnings other than Mother's ha'pennies were a shilling a day at potato-picking (from about seven till half-past five) and then a few weeks at swede cleaning at the same rate of pay, and with that came the end of my agricultural employment for life. I'd had more than enough. The cold! Pulling swedes with the frost on them first thing in the morning . . .

Now comes the time when I had to leave home and go to Blenheim for good. My mother gave me a nice box of clothes — and a shilling. "There you are," she said, pressing it into my hand, "take this and be a good little boy." And I can truthfully say that was all the money I ever had from my parents the whole of my life.

Service at Blenheim

My great-grandfather, grandfather and father, all, in their times, worked at Blenheim Palace, and now I too found myself being interviewed by the steward.

"What's your name?" he asked.

"Gerald, sir."

"What?"

"Gerald, sir."

"Gerald? Oh no, that won't do. We will call you Johnny."

And Johnny I have been from that day fifty years ago to this. The steward took me on to work the palace telephone exchange, and I can tell you, when I found I was in charge of thirty-seven lines connecting the Duke with his estate, I was more than a little nervous. The Duke was all right, but he could certainly make one tremble and when he came round with the steward on his monthly inspection you'd most likely hear a roar and think that what was coming down the passage was a giant.

Besides seeing to the telephone I was hall-boy, which meant looking after the under-servants' hall, laying their meals, and so on. My pay was £12 a year and two suits of morning clothes made of that pepper-and-salt stuff which nearly all servants at that time had to wear. My hours were 7 till 11, most of the time on the go, with two afternoons and evenings off a week. When I was off I was off and away home or fishing in the lake, but when footmen were off duty they were still on call for carriage-work, work which was not popular at any time because the hats they had to wear to take their places on the carriage spoilt their hair, and when they returned the whole business of setting and powdering had to be gone through again. Oh yes, to be a footman in those days, with a place worth calling a place, you had to powder every day and that meant washing your hair with soap, combing it out, getting it set in waves and then powdering it. You never dried your hair but left it to set like cement. The powder you mixed yourself, buying violet powder from the chemist's and mixing it with flour. The powdering allowance for footmen was two guineas a year.

There was never any question of my powdering at Blenheim because, since no liveried servant was engaged there unless he was six feet or over (I was five foot nine), I could never be promoted. Later on though in other mansions powdering went with my job, and I for one am heartily glad that the practice has since been abolished. It is most uncomfortable and to my way of thinking should never be asked of any human being. But honestly, I don't think the gentry realized

181

what you went through doing this kind of thing. Most of the footmen at Blenheim were well over six feet and their uniform consisted of maroon plush breeches, maroon coat and waistcoat with silver braid, flesh-coloured silk stockings and patent shoes with silver buckles.

The inside staff of the palace was normally from thirty-six to forty, and at busy times very many more, for of course every visitor brought a maid, a lady as often as not bringing a special footman to clean her boots and shoes; and the visitors' servants made quite as much work as the gentry themselves. The outside staff numbered forty to fifty, and there was also the hunting department, carried on at the home farm at Bladon with a staff of about a dozen. Sixteen to twenty horses (including six Scots Greys) were kept for hunting and there were some twenty carriage horses, bays, beautiful things. Then there was the electrician's staff of four, two house carpenters and two decorators who spent nearly all their time helping themselves to flowers from the pleasure grounds and arranging them. They were clever though. I shall always remember that snow scene of theirs, for I never saw anything more wonderful of its kind. Everything you looked at in the palace that night was white and sparkling as it would be in the winter woods, even to the little birds in the trees. But for special occasions the centrepiece for the dinner table was always the same. It was a massive, solid silver affair representing the first Duke of Marlborough writing despatches at the battle of Blenheim. It took two strong men to lift it.

Another sort of worker was the great Mr. Perkins of Birmingham who was summoned nearly every week-end to play the palace organ in the Long Library (usually after dinner). But he was treated as one of their own people.

A day I shall always remember was when the Duke brought his bride — Miss Consuelo Vanderbilt as she had been — back from their honeymoon in Egypt. Woodstock, of course, was smothered in flags, and at the station the bays were taken from the shafts and the carriage, with our master and mistress, drawn by the estate men to the town hall and from there to the palace in triumph. It was a great thing for me to stand there and see them brought home in such style and when the Duchess stepped down from the carriage you might almost have heard us gasp at how young and how beautiful she was. And she was as good as she was beautiful too. In fact, she would go out of her way to be kind to everyone, and of course she was idolised. At Christmas, for instance, she saw to it personally that everyone in the villages belonging to Blenheim had a blanket or a pig or a ton of coal or whatever it was they wanted. She was a great lady.

The Duchess had brought with her from Egypt a black pageboy, a Mohammedan, who came to be known as Mike. Not a word of English could he speak when he arrived, and yet in six months he was word perfect. In fact, he could speak too well, for he swore like a trooper. Did I say he was a Mohammedan? Yes, and at first he would eat no pork. He was persuaded to try it though, and liked it so much he ate of it heartily

183

ever after. I can tell you I had some very fine battles and stand-up fights with that blackamoor, and me being a rather powerful boy, used to give him a darn good hiding. Oh, but he was a nineter though, and he'd whip out a knife too as soon as look at you.

One day we were in our boys' pantry having a bit of lunch when something happened, and before I knew what he was about the black boy had hit me on the head with a beer jug. Of course I flew at him and while we were fighting the housekeeper came in and cried out, "Oh Johnny, Johnny, what are you doing?" and I said "Yes, and I'll kill the little b— I will"; but she parted us and made us promise not to fight again.

No sooner had she gone though than I was at him for another go and landed him a black eye. Now that's a thing I don't think many can have seen — a black boy with a black eye — but there it was, as good a black eye as ever you saw, spoiling his fine looks at table and making him wish he'd never touched Johnny Horne nor the beer jug.

Unluckily for me — and perhaps for him too — Mike and me shared a bedroom, so neither of us had very peaceful nights; for even if we weren't fighting each other, we were never safe from the pranks of the footmen. They were devils, those footmen, and if we locked the door they broke it open. One night they ran in and dragging us both from our beds put blacking all over my face and blanco all over the blackamoor's. It seems funny enough now, but certainly there were times when their pranks went too far, and although I never complained to anyone about them I did make up my mind that if ever I rose as far as butler I would make it my business to see that no footman under me interfered with my boys.

The black page's work was to sit in the front hall with a footman, from ten till six or seven, so as to be there to let anyone in or out. On special occasions he would stand behind the Duchess's chair at dinner, but of course he did no waiting. On those occasions he was always dressed in the elaborate uniform of his country, one outfit yellow, the other scarlet: turban, tunic, skirt and tasselled sash. He looked very picturesque, I'll say that much, but he was a dangerous customer all the same. As time went on I think the Duke returned him to his native land.

Naturally the Duke and Duchess entertained very lavishly. Wonderful week-end parties they gave, with tea in the boathouse and the Blue Hungarian Band from London to play at dinner, not to mention Mr. Perkins' organ playing afterwards. But the greatest occasion of all during my time at Blenheim was the visit of the late King Edward, then Prince of Wales, and the Princess. The Princess Victoria was also of the party, as were Prince and Princess Charles of Denmark, and they all stayed several days for the shooting. Altogether there were thirty-six guests, and on the evening of their arrival we had first a torchlight procession (and very pretty it looked crossing the lake by the old stone bridge) and then a banquet. Well, some of us were given permission to go up on the balcony that night and look down into the front hall where at one long table they were dining, and of course

I went up and looked down and there it was, all gleaming with wealth. I think the first thing that struck me was the flashing headgears of the ladies. The Blue Hungarian was playing, and there was the Prince himself looking really royal and magnificent in military uniform. The table was laid, of course, with the silver gilt service, the old silver duke busy writing as usual in the very middle of it all and the royal footmen waiting side by side with our own.

Shooting parties at Blenheim were elaborate affairs and this royal party was far from being an exception. Sixteen to twenty keepers were always kept; and the food, sent out in padded baskets was reheated on a stove when it reached the luncheon tent. To prevent accidents all the beaters were dressed in white smocks and red tam-o'-shanters. The keepers were very smart in Irish green velvet for their coats and vests with brass buttons, brown breeches and leggings and black billycock hats. The head keeper was distinguished by a hat like Mr. Churchill's. (It was at Blenheim that we once had the record shoot of the world, five guns shooting 7,500 rabbits in one day. One of the guns that day was the Duke, another Prince Dulep Singh, a frequent visitor, as was also Mr. Winston Churchill with his mother, but he usually went out riding.)

When the royal visit came to an end, as you can imagine, everyone was more or less exhausted, so the Duke and Duchess decided to go away and give us all a complete rest. They had been gone only one day when fire broke out in the roof of the saloon. Luckily the palace fire brigade had been training that morning and had only just left for their quarters. One of the decorators came running to me and calling "Johnny, there's a fire! Ring the bell!" You bet I tugged with a will and within five minutes the brigade was at the front door and pumping away with their old steamer* and manual to the tune of 60,000 gallons an hour.

The thing that tickled me at the time was the panic of the housekeeper. I can see her now as she rushes into the front hall, and, throwing her arms round a statue that must have weighed five hundredweight if it weighed a pound, tries to carry it off. The steward too was in a dither and took a knife to cut down the dining-room tapestries. The land steward came in though, and before he could do much, stopped him. Everything movable was cleared from the saloon and put on the lawn. The fire had started from a beam in the chimney which must have been smouldering all the time the royal party was with us.

But I shall always remember the part I played in the fire. I don't mean ringing the bell, though that was jolly enough. No, I mean sweeping the water downstairs when the fire was out. Along came the water, you see, like a great dirty river to where me and Mike, the black page, were standing with our brooms at the top of the basement stairs. As you can guess, nothing gave us more enjoyment than getting our feet into plenty of

* I have recently seen this elegant appliance. It has, painted on each side of the driver's box, a ducal coronet, and in large gold capitals across the centre panel the word BLENHEIM. — D. B. G.

water, and for nearly an hour that day we both had the time of our lives, yelling in English and in what I suppose was Egyptian as with all our strength and enthusiasm we helped the water downstairs.

The fire had done little damage, the water a great deal. The brigade stayed on and I had to get them food and beer. Still they stayed, enjoying themselves no end, till it all turned into a singsong right up to midnight and everyone went to bed at last thoroughly happy. What's more the insurance company sent us all a reward, the firemen a fiver each, our men a pound and myself fifteen shillings — a tremendous sum to me in those days.

Now I must tell you that like most men-servants we at Blenheim were given to gambling. Well, one evening six or seven of us were sitting at it in the servants' hall when my father, as was his weekly custom, came along and asked me for my washing. Now father was a good-living man, and in our home gambling was not of course to be thought of. But he had me fair and square this time, for there we all were, very interested playing nap and although directly I saw how it was I dabbed my hand over my money (and there was quite a lot of it too), I knew he wasn't as blind as all that.

"Johnny, let me have your washing, will you?" he said, quiet enough. Everyone stopped playing and looked at each other, but no one said anything nor made a move. At last father said:

"Come on, I can't stand here all night;" so I said, "All right, Dad," and stood up — and there was my money staring him in the face.

Though he said nothing about it then, I knew well enough I was for it. So in the morning I went fishing in the lake and had the luck to land an eight-pound pike. I thought, now if I give this to my father it will square matters nicely. So up I went to his workshop and said, "Dad, I've got a fish for you." And "Yes," he said, very solemn, "and do you know, my boy, you're going the right way to Hell?" Yes, that was the straightest talk he ever gave me, but in spite of it I played whenever I could.

But the worst thing I remember happening through gambling, while I was in the Duke's employment, occurred one winter's day when we were returning from Sysonby, the Duke's hunting lodge at Melton Mowbray. Only certain of the staff would accompany him there: the groom of the chambers, two footmen, three housemaids, three in the kitchen, an odd man and myself, with of course the stud groom, second horseman and stable helpers. A special train took the lot of us, including the horses, both ways. On the journey we all played nap and enjoyed it, but on the day I'm telling you about, when they opened the horse vans at Woodstock, there was one of us at least who wished he'd sat with the hunters instead. One of the Duke's lovely Scots Greys had hanged itself; been scared by the noise of the train or something and pulled and kept pulling on its halter till it was strangled. Well of course it was a terrible blow for the stableman in charge and took a bit of explaining. The Duke took it all in good part though, and the thing was looked on as just an unfortunate happening.

To most of us working there, Blenheim was the world, and not so small a world either, the palace itself covering three acres and the estate including most of Woodstock and the surrounding villages.

Altogether I was there three and a half years, and I must say it was a most wonderful place, and in spite of all I had to put up with from footmen and so on, I was most happy and left only to better my position. (For being under six feet, as I've said, it was useless to hope for promotion there.)

But where could you go in those days? What could you do with your free time? You had to make your own amusement, and it's no wonder there was so much drinking and gambling. Trains were bad, there were no buses; so going into Oxford meant a slow ride by pony and trap. When you got there you went to a pub and looked at pretty pictures through a telescope. Were they indecent? Well no, but as near as they could go without being indecent. True, at Blenheim there was fishing in the lake, and I took full advantage of it. Once I caught a four pound eel and mother made eel pie, and a very welcome dinner it made us. The Duke and Duchess were away at the time and we were on board wages: twelve shillings, vegetables, milk, and half a pound of butter a week. Did we ever take to poaching? No, I never did. It was far too risky.

You ask what I think about gentleman's service to-day? Well of course to-day what servants there are can be off to the pictures and do pretty much as they like. I'm sorry to see some of the old ways go all the same. In my time, for instance, it was always the thing for

190

the under-servants to call the steward "Sir" and the housekeeper "Mam." But there, years ago servants were the best-spoken and the best-trained of any working folk in the country. In those days the steward and the housekeeper very often had more authority with the under-servants than the gentry themselves. Their word was law. To-day they have very little authority and little respect is paid them. And then look how ideas on the age of a manservant have changed. The gentry's view used to be that until you were forty you could have no authority; and they were quite willing to keep you until you were eighty. They looked upon a man of years as one to be trusted, but now, why 'pon me sammy, they wouldn't look at you if you'd just turned sixty! Yes, it has all changed and to any youngster thinking of gentleman's service to-day I'd say for girls, yes, a grand thing, for they get more freedom now than ever they got; but for men, no. Who wants butlers to-day? People can't pay them a worthwhile wage and tipping's nothing like what it was. Why, the whole time I did valeting, I can tell you this, I never got less than a bit of gold. You could hardly expect that today!

(III) BLENHEIM TO-DAY

As you walk down the buttercup meadow from our village to Duke's Wood you can look over the tops of the young ashes and hazels, right across the fields beyond, to a much older wood of oak and beech, chestnut and cedar, among which, on the skyline, you may just distinguish the pinnacles of "that golden

191

Italian palace" (as Lady Eleanor Smith called it), which is Blenheim.

To the left of those pinnacles, and still "bosom'd high in tufted trees," you see a machicolated tower which you may easily take for part of a private chapel. Walk towards it and, like the house in "Through the Looking Glass," it seems to recede, soon to submerge completely in a sea of oaks, while you yourself may be floundering in a bog where, among alder and butter-burr, the would-be modest river Glyme is making its abused and tedious way to join the Evenlode. Renounce then all idea of getting anywhere, wander aimlessly in the park and sooner or later you will stumble upon a tower you recognize and, boldly knocking, find yourself at that hunting-lodge where John Wilmot, second Earl of Rochester, poet and satirist, died, one summer's night, at the miserably early age of thirty-three.

High Lodge, a restored, gothicized relic, standing beside pleasant ponds and looking from its wooded hill clear across river and field and wood to Oxford, eight miles off, seems a place where it might be well enough to die but infinitely more agreeable to go on living. And indeed we know that as the young earl, banished and ill and "beginning to show signs of a more serious temper," looked from his bedroom window towards Wadham, where he had taken his M.A. at fourteen, he had no kind feelings for a court which could wear a poet to a ravelling when he had lived but half a life and that he was "sorry he had lived so as to waste his strength so soon."

Nearly two hundred and seventy years after Rochester's death his bed, with its coarse yellow hangings, survives him, as does also, though barely, the chair upon which, until recently, one might see his sword. There is nothing of the poet, though, not even quill or parchment in that long unlived-in room, nor in any of those antler-hung chambers with their creepered windows and floors littered with dead bats and tortoiseshell butterflies. It is better to take the stair to the roof and standing on the leads look around you — towards Oxford or distant Wychwood, or westward to Duke's Wood and the tall, sunlit spire rising behind it . . . Is not that enough to turn almost any man poet?*

Downstairs, in direct contrast to the barrenness of the rooms above, you see a bright fire burning merrily in a cosy kitchen that might belong to any cottage where the housewife knows how to make a grate sparkle and an old-fashioned oven give of its toothsome best. It is the kind of interior which will be known to our grandchildren only through the small, shiny pages of their Beatrix Potters and makes one wonder how it is that where centuries ago the whole hunting-box was barely big enough for one nobleman and his flock of servants, to-day a mere corner of the shell does very nicely for two families which, with no suggestion of overcrowding, look to be living a great deal more comfortably and warmly than did the exiled earl.

* Some notes on the life and death of the Earl of Rochester are added in the form of an appendix at the end of this chapter.

Obviously, in these crabbed times, to inhabit part only of a large house, or, where practicable, to share it, is the sensible thing; and in the palace itself we find the ducal family living in the east wing, while the rest is, for the time being, devoted to the gargantuan needs of a government department.

To most modern eyes the outside of the palace, seen head-on, undoubtedly comes as a shock. Some say frankly that it reminds them of Euston station; others that it has character, speaks forcefully of a past age, and is, with its knobs and balls and balconies and its chatty statues perched here and there upon balustrades, quite unlike anything else they have seen in any part of the world. Of these latter, George III was probably the first, and the most tactful, when turning to his wife and daughters he said, "We have nothing to equal this."

But there is no need to look at the palace in this way. John Betjeman, writing of Vanbrugh's "exuberant architecture," says, "He (Vanbrugh) thought of the palace as something to be seen square-on at the end of a straight avenue. Capability Brown thought that it should be glimpsed only partially as an irregular arrangement of towers and vertical objects, seen between carefully planted and irregular groups of beeches from different levels. He therefore designed the main approach from the town of Woodstock by a triumphal gateway . . . and there is no doubt that the first view of the palace, lake, and bridge, seen from there, is the most impressive. This was the view Turner painted."

194

Inside the palace, in that sixty-seven foot high entrance hall where royalty feasted, it is not at the moment easy to picture the sparkling scene Johnny Horne described. Gone is the long table he looked down on, "all gleaming with wealth," gone the "flashing headgears of the ladies," the uniforms, the silver-gilt service, the Blue Hungarian Band, and in their place one sees a draughty-looking, temporary office, like a set for It Pays to Advertise lowered on to a stage already prepared for *Götterdämmerung*.

As is so often the case in these vast show-places it is the detail that appeals. Look, for instance, at the lock on the huge front doors. There is no keyhole to be seen. Touch a spring and the lock's own little "church" doors fly open, inviting you to insert the massive steel key; and as your fingers close round it you find yourself clasping a fat ducal coronet.

Then step out into the portico and look up at the coffered ceiling. Your gaze is met and returned by six gigantic eyes, the two largest well over a yard wide, three blue and three brown, short-lashed, heavy-lidded, each surrounded by a multiple rayed sunburst and framed in a heavy gilt frame. They are said to have been painted at the express order of a duchess, though no one seems to know why. Was the doorkeeper apt to "sit down on the job," and was this his mistress's notion of corrective, on the lines of Genesis xvi. 13?

Of the rest of what I have seen within the palace (I have not seen all the private apartments) I remember three things: the Sargent of the late Duke's family (the poise and serene beauty of the dark duchess Consuelo); the raised velvet wallpapers; and the organ at the far end of the Long (white) Library, an organ of sixty-four ivory stops bearing such seraphic names as

Claribel Flute	Dulciana Choir
Flageolet Swell	Violoncello Pedale
Clarion	Corno di Bassetto Choir
Ophicleide Pedale	Quint Octaviente
Tromba	Contra Hautboy Swell
Cor Anglais Choir	Piccolo Choir

and the commemoration

> In memory of happy days and as a
> tribute to this glorious home we
> leave thy voice to speak within
> these walls in years to come,
> when ours are still
> L.M.   1891   M.M.

Sarah Jennings, the first Duchess, considered the palace an uncomfortable place to live in, and, as you may remember, dismissed the architect long before it was finished. The final quarrel occurred after Vanbrugh, in one of those expansive moments so frequent with him, had decided to throw across the diminutive Glyme the largest spanned stone-built arch in Britain, if not in Europe, at a cost of twenty thousand pounds. He was given his way and his notice, but the bridge remained, bestriding the narrow Glyme like a colossus and offending the Duchess's sight whenever she looked in that direction or went out for a drive.* Short of tearing down the bridge, a many-roomed mansion in itself, there was only one thing to do: make the Glyme perform to scale, "swell to a lake the scant, penurious rill," so that all three arches, instead of only the middle one, should be reflected in one vast lake, even if it meant that one could no longer enter the rooms. For such an enterprise there was but one man — Capability Brown — and he did indeed swell the rill to a lake of 120 acres, making, as he boasted, the Thames look like a small stream and afterwards sending the contorted Glyme down an elaborate cascade, for all the world like a performing seal or, in fact, like almost anything but the sedate rivulet it originally must have been.

To-day, one pier is accessible only by boat or when the lake is frozen. The other may sometimes be entered, but one would not penetrate far without a torch. Indeed, had it not been for two little ragamuffins who, on that first visit, most obligingly lit our way, I might never have explored it so thoroughly myself, nor

* "The enormous arch," says Ballard in his "Chronicles of the Royal Borough of Woodstock," spanned a little rivulet scarcely ten feet broad; which prompted Pope to compose the epigram:
The minnows at you, as this vast arch they pass
Cry 'How like whales we look, thanks to your Grace!'
By enlarging the lake, Capability Brown, in Boswell's phrase, 'drowned the epigram.'"

seen the round rooms, nor written the story (such as it is) of *Fairfax the Squirrel*.

Almost directly you have passed under the pier archway leading into the bridge you turn right and climb a damp, twisting stair to a long, dark passage, remarkable for its height (about seven feet) and, in winter, for its wealth of hibernating butterflies, spiders and mosquitoes. The rubble floor is uneven, but keeping the beam down and minding your step you let the passage lead you right and then left again, when you see light streaming in from each side and wonder which to explore first. You soon find that both sides are alike, having the same sort of rough corridor leading to a delightful little round room, high, the pale walls dappled with light reflected from the lake and the large, uncasemented windows, with wide sills, giving on the south-west to that great expanse of water which ends in the Cascade, and on the east to Elizabeth's Island and, perched above that part of the lake which stretches away behind it, groups of trees and grey, creeper-covered buildings clustered around the square tower of Woodstock Church.

I have said that except for their outlooks the two round rooms are the same, but there is one other difference: that on the Cascade side has what was once a fireplace and a chimney; though in accordance with Vanbrugh's policy, which applies to the palace, there is no chimney to be seen from outside.

The tale goes that the bridge was once used as a cool retreat in summer; but one wonders to what extent it

was ever furnished and lived in, if at all.* Certainly
there was never a more fertile spot for legend, and the
stories told about the bridge are rivalled only by those
about the Fair Rosamund and the labyrinth which is
said to have led Henry II's queen to the secret bower
when she (Rosamund) was careless enough to drop a
ball of silk. And indeed there are days when, sitting on
the sill and watching the martins fix their nests to the
bridge face, or looking down into inaccessible rooms
where water-weeds grow, or following the path the sun
makes towards the island and losing it in the dense
reflection of its poplars, it is easy to believe anything,

* "In this bridge are various apartments, some with fireplaces
which have never been fitted up, though for summer retreats
they would be extremely pleasant. On the side next Blenheim
they are inaccessible since the expansion of the lake. In some
of these dark and unexplored recesses it is not impossible that
one or more species of the swallow tribe find a winter retreat
and lie in a torpid state till the return of spring. This is certain,
that they have been noticed skimming the lake as early as any
have been discovered on the sea coasts. One season a *white*
swallow was seen there for a considerable time."
— *From Dr. Mavor's famous guide to Blenheim* (1789). *The
theory of swallows and their kind hibernating in such places was, of
course, a popular fallacy, investigated by Gilbert White.*

"Four houses are to be at each corner of the bridge; but that
which makes it so much prettier than London Bridge is, that
you may set in six rooms and look out at window into the high
road while the coaches are driving over your head." — *Sarah
Jennings, first Duchess of Marlborough, in a letter of bitter
complaint to Mrs. Clayton.*

199

till one catches oneself seriously contemplating a search for the "lost" passage leading from bridge-house to island and from island to hidden room somewhere among the heavy tapestries in the palace.

Decidedly, to the average more or less staid grown-up, the bridge-house is exciting. To a small boy it must surely mean dreams come true: his galleon, his smugglers' cave, his robbers' lair. It is vast, mysterious, dark and watery, semi-private, not too easy of access and none too safe — what more could the most daring and unreasonable child expect? Even a five-year-old who has explored the bridge often may be heard to protest when it's time to go home, "But I wish I could live here all my life, in these round rooms."

But what is so enchanting about the whole of Blenheim, bridge, park and all, is that there never seems an end to its surprises, both great and small. The first and I suppose the greatest is when, having passed between the high walls and beneath the triumphal arch, the world opens out suddenly to an immense green and gold tapestry, and with a quite foreign and unwonted sense of freedom you step straight into the spaciousness of another age. As Mavor, in the style of his day, remarked, "The sublime predominates in a very high degree, and frigid indeed must that taste be which will not feel and confess the energy of the scene." At any season it is indeed more than impressive, though personally I would choose autumn, when the poplars on Elizabeth's Island are surrounded by dark crimson dogwood and the lake is thickly dotted with waterfowl (the mallard rise *en masse* with a noise like heavy applause): or possibly midwinter when skaters — bright blobs of colour, as you look down on them — weave in and out aimlessly, like windblown stragglers from a bunch of toy balloons.

My own first introduction to Blenheim — as though to break it gently — was by way of the Bladon Gate, an approach gentle and gradual. There is nothing pretentious there. Of the palace one sees only the upper storeys and a farrago of towers flanked by tall trees; while the river Glyme, having as it were been through the hoop (the lake bridge) and over the falls (the Cascade) and picked its way amid sedge and spearwort to flow quietly beneath a modest and very beautiful stone bridge, pauses and rests a moment, in the form of a small, wild lake, before thankfully reverting to its natural size in preparation for its meeting with the Evenlode.

Sloping up from the palace side of that lake is close-cropped pasture bearing here and there a neat clump of copper beech or silver fir representing, it is said, regiments at the battle of Blenheim. For my part they may stand for squads of police or battalions of chambermaids. They are beautiful in themselves. Furthermore, one at least of the round dumps, the one Roger has christened Snow Copse, is magically productive, presenting us at odd times with a fungus as neat and round as itself and in flavour excelling that of the common *Psalliota campestris*. I mean, of course, the hedge mushroom, a delicacy few know, and even fewer — such being the superstition about fungus beneath trees — dare to touch; and it is their sudden profuse occurrence, at times when no field mushroom is to be found, that to me makes them characteristic of Blenheim in mystery, bounty and surprise.

Even so I must own that I once took a risk with these mushrooms and was let off more lightly than I deserved. It so happened that I was in a hurry (always a mistake when mushrooming or blackberrying), and, arrived in the copse, found all its mushrooms gathered but abandoned in a heap at the foot of a tree. With muttered thanks to good fairies and guardian angels I bundled them into a large red handkerchief and hurried home. . . . Cut, as the film people say, to 3a.m. next morning when I woke in violent pain. "Mushrooms?" said J. "Toadstools?" said I. "Not Deathcap?" she gasped. But no, it wasn't. After some hours the pain went; and on many occasions since, the produce of Snow Copse, gathered at first hand, has afforded us much painless delight.

But there is, as I have said, no end to these for the most part pleasant small surprises at Blenheim; they cannot be catalogued. Where else, for example, may one see in August a giant beech *dripping* with small birds? I stood beneath it while the sun shone through and revealed hundreds of the commoner tits and finches which with willow-wrens, nuthatches and others were everywhere in silent pursuit of a hatch of insects, so that it was hard to tell which were birds and which leaves.

Where else would one come upon an antler sticking up from the midst of a swamp and, clearing the ground, discover it to be attached to a flat, *iron* deer which was once, in its upright position, part of a romantic "prospect"?

Suddenly in that same swamp we chanced on a patch like a wild garden, studded with water forget-me-not, watermint, ragged robin, spotted orchis and its rich cousin the marsh orchis in its two so different forms of reddish purple and rose-pink.

It was suddenly, too, that I came across that small lake-island crossed to with the help of a flattened kettle, where I watched the nuthatch and the flycatcher watched me.

Sometimes it is a sound which gives the first hint of coming surprises, as when we heard the rush of water and, softly trespassing, saw for the first time, from that fragile Swiss bridge, the green boulders and great dripping beards of moss over which gushes Capability's cascade.

Nowhere else have I seen a crested grebe blithely sitting entirely without cover, on its own little lake-island; nor martins building, as though for perpetual summer, on August 24th! Even the dragonflies at Blenheim seem strangely confiding, one with wings of pale amber letting me coax it from a lakeside nettle on to my finger and show it to a Shropshire farmer's daughter who happened to be with us. ("They're quiet, aren't they?" she said.)

The very trees here are different, immense cedars (sometimes seen *through* cardinal willows), setting the scale, and pale, feather leaved exotics towering behind prunus and willow and purple hazel, to make bands of restful colour and all reflected, as like as not, in pond or lake. The cedars, like venerable celebrities, are impossible to imagine young; though not even they bring home the age of the park as tellingly as do the oaks in the deer park about High Lodge. It was of one of those hoary grotesques, hollow and twisted and calloused, worn by Time into huge holes, *à la* Arthur Rackham, that Roger said, "It looks as though it would follow you out with all those mouths . . . including a teapot-mouth." From the heart of one of its neighbours we were shown wood containing a lump of lead thought to have entered the sapling at about the time when bullets were invented.

Often one appears to have the whole park to oneself, lakes, cedars and all, admission free, rent free, tax free, and no charge for upkeep — what a wonderful arrangement! Even a duke, one feels, is less to be envied, for he can scarcely pass a broken gate without its adding to his burdens or a weed-choked lake without counting the cost of getting it cleared. And it is true that to some extent this most formal of parks, with its ha-has and straight avenues, its rose gardens and clipped yew, has had to be let run wild — greatly, as I see it, to its advantage; though that Mr. Wise who did so much of the planning with the first Duke, must revolve in his grave. ("For the Gardening and Plantations," wrote the campaigning Duke on the eve of battle, "I am at ease, being very sure that Mr. Wise will bee dilligent.")

To-day, Handsome Jack Churchill, as a massive leaden statue in Roman battle-dress, looks stonily from his 130-foot Doric column, seeing nothing of the changes, neither weeds nor army huts nor the strangers within his gates. Yet while he lived he had the tenderest feelings for home . . .

"We have for these last ten days had extreame hot weather," he wrote from camp to his duchess in the summer of 1708, "which I hope may give you good peaches at Woodstock, wher I shou'd be better pleas'd to eat even the worst that were ever tasted than the good ones we have here, for every day of my life I grow more impatient for quiet."

And it is as much for quiet as for beauty and unexpectedness that that eccentric, the quiet man, prizes his freedom of Blenheim to-day, whether in the open parklands or in the wilder and more secret parts, as for instance where the Glyme's subterranean tributary leaps from cedar-shaded ground to join the Evenlode. In the hush of an autumn evening, when the reflected cedars "in fading deeps of light" seem about to let loose the darkness, it does indeed seem enchanted land, so that I for one would never be astonished to find myself for a few magical moments (as did those two lucky and learned women at Versailles*) in another age. Would one, then, witness the grim progress of a dusty leather coach pulled by tired horses up the rough track to High Lodge (within, in agony, the young Earl of Rochester returning from Somerset to die?). Or surprise the second Henry at

* "An Adventure," by Charlotte Moberly and Eleanor Jourdain (Faber).

205

Fair Rosamund's bower? Perhaps one would catch Elizabeth scrawling with diamond on the pane of the old manor gatehouse(it stood not far from the Glyme), where Sister Mary imprisoned her —

> Much suspected of me
> Nothing proved can be
> Quoth Elizabeth pris'ner.

Or see Sarah Jennings' men demolishing the remains of that same Woodstock Manor, which "offended her eyes." Again, it might be in times far more recent, times Johnny Horne tells of, to be a witness to the Duchess's return from her Egyptian honeymoon (the citizens of Woodstock drawing the ducal carriage and agog at her beauty and the blackness of Mike, the Mohammedan page). Or would one be looking down on that royal banquet or watching the torchlight procession reflected in the lake?

However it might be, though more than content with the park as it is, I shall continue to go prepared for such phenomena. As Jefferies says, there is "nothing astonishing in what are called miracles. The wonder rather is that they do not happen frequently. Only those who are mesmerized by matter can find a difficulty in such events . . . It is matter which is the supernatural and difficult of understanding."

APPENDIX

THE EARL OF ROCHESTER

John Wilmot, second Earl of Rochester, was born at
Ditchley, Oxfordshire, in April, 1647, and began his
education at Burford Grammar School. At the age of
fourteen he took his M.A. at Wadham, and soon after,
having as it were exhausted Oxford, travelled with a
tutor in Italy and France, studying the while to such
effect that while still in his teens he established a
reputation, for what it was worth in those days, as the
greatest scholar among all the nobility.

In a less licentious reign than Charles II's he might
well have maintained it. As it was, "of a graceful and
well-shaped person, tall and well made if not a little too
slender; exactly well bred; his conversation easy and
obliging, with a strange vivacity of thought and vigour
of expression" (*vide* Bishop Burnet), he at once found
favour at Court, and, after serving a while with the
Fleet and distinguishing himself against the Dutch by
"uncommon intrepidity," was made a Gentleman of
the Bedchamber, and, in time, Comptroller of
Woodstock Park and Keeper of the King's Hawks.

So far so good. But it was, as Dr. Burnet remarks, a
loose and lewd age, and turning to Johnson's "Lives,"
one sees that as Rochester "excelled in that noisy and
licentious merriment which wine incites, his
companions eagerly encouraged him in excess, and he
willingly indulged in it till, as he confessed to Dr.

Burnet, he was for five years together continually drunk or so much inflamed by frequent ebriety as in no instance to be master of himself."

It is obvious that on many an occasion wine and a doubtful sense of humour got the better of the earl's otherwise excellent intellect and good sense. His pranks included masquerading as a tinker at Burford (he knocked the bottoms out of their kettles but afterwards sent them new ones) and as a mountebank (in the manner of Volpone) on Tower Hill; as a consequence of which he came to be called the Mad Earl. Less funny were the more vicious and violent of his escapades — as, for instance, the beating up of Dryden in Covent Garden — and the more schoolboyish of his rhymes aimed at the king.

As each new piece of ribaldry made its circuitous way towards its royal objective, bags would be packed and the coach made ready in anticipation of yet another enforced sixty-mile journey, over terrible roads, to High Lodge, Woodstock, for him who came to sign himself "your Country Acquaintance." Yet again he would, says Johnson, "retire into the country and amuse himself with writing libels in which he did not pretend to confine himself to truth." On an average these dismissals from Court are said to have occurred once a year.

But Rochester was by no means the only one of his circle to find libel (except upon oneself) amusing. It was enough for him to leave Court for Woodstock, to set a multitude of tongues wagging so that everything he did, no matter how patently blameless, became cause for scandal among courtiers incapable and unwishful of talking and thinking anything else. One such rumour spoke of his having run about Woodstock Park with his friends, "naked and on the Sabbath." Taxed with which he replied, "For the hideous Deportment which you have heard of so much is true, that we went into the River somewhat late in the Year and had a Frisk for forty yards in the Meadow, to dry ourselves. I will appeal to the King and the Duke, If they had not done as much; nay, my Lord-chancellor and the Archbishops both, when they were Schoolboys?"

As a man of family (there were three daughters and a son who died a few months after his father) Rochester was by no means a pattern. His "most neglected Wife," Elizabeth Mallet, a Papist, was not only for months at a time denied the company of her lord but treated to that of his mother, a Puritan of very determined mind. The letters from Rochester to Elizabeth are brief and full of excuses. Such of hers as survive read pitifully.

He had been on his way to his wife's estate in Somerset when, while on horseback, he was overcome by violent pain and forced to turn back. Suffering from internal inflammation, "with very great difficulty he endured a return to the Ranger's Lodge at Woodstock, by coach." It was April, 1680 (he died in July), but there was still the same flippant sprightliness in his letters to his friend Henry Savile. "It is a miraculous thing," he remarks, "when a Man half in the Grave cannot leave off playing the Fool and the Buffoon; but so it falls out to my Comfort; for at this Moment I am in a damn'd Relapse brought on by a Feaver, the Stone and some ten Diseases more, which have deprived me of the Power of crawling, which I happily enjoy'd some Days ago; and now I fear I must fall, that it may be fulfilled which was long since written for Instruction in a good old Ballad —

> But he who lives not Wise and Sober
> Falls with the Leaf still in October,

about which time, in all probability, there may be a period added to the ridiculous being of
your humble Servant,
ROCHESTER."

His mind had, however, its serious side. Much of the previous winter he had spent closeted with his old friend Bishop Burnet, and although at that time discussion on religious belief had failed to convince him, he had clearly given the matter much thought and continued to do so. It is not altogether surprising, then, that on June 25th, "with his own Hand, at Twelve at Night," the wretched earl wrote from High Lodge his urgent and celebrated last letter to Burnet, summoning him to his bedside forthwith. Burnet came and had the satisfaction of witnessing Rochester's deathbed confession and repentance to which he (the bishop) attested the sincerity.

Both countesses, wife and mother, were at the bedside and towards the end Rochester, according to his confessor, "expressed so much tenderness and kindness to his lady that as it easily effaced the remembrance of everything wherein he had been in fault formerly, so it drew from her the most passionate care and concern for him that was possible."

Of the final scene St. Evremont records:

"The continual Course of Drinking and a perpetual Decay of his Spirits in Love and Writing had entirely broken his Constitution and brought him into a Consumption of which, after a lingering Sickness, he died at the Lodge in Woodstock Park on the 26th of July, 1680 at Two in the Morning, without any Pangs at all, Nature being spent and all the Food of Life quite gone, in the third and thirtieth Year of his Age."

He had, says Burnet, "run round the whole circle of luxury"; and, adds Dr. Johnson, "blazed out his youth and his health in lavish voluptuousness till he had exhausted the fund of life and reduced himself to a state of weakness and decay."

As the earl lay dying he directed that the History of the Intrigues of the Court, upon which he had been engaged, should be burned, and this was done. Some, including Horace Walpole, have thought it a pity that the same fate was not meted out to the whole of Rochester's works. Johnson, on the other hand, "found in all his works sprightliness and vigour and . . . tokens of a mind which study might have carried to excellence

. . . And what more," adds the doctor, "can be expected of a life spent in ostentatious contempt of regularity and ended before the abilities of many other men began to be displayed?"

CHAPTER
FIVE

Between Thames and Windrush

VIOLET GROWERS
(i) Cornish Preliminary

On a day in April, cycling through an Oxfordshire village, Stanton Harcourt,* that was new to me, I smelt

---

* In the days of Edward VI the Lord of Stanton Harcourt, at any time when the snow should lie for the space of two days, was obliged to find four browsers for the purpose of furnishing provisions for the deer in Woodstock Park (now part of Blenheim). The King's bailiff gave warning of the browsers being wanted by blowing a horn at the Manor gate, whereupon he was to be served with a caste of bread, a gallon of ale and a piece of cheese. For this Lord Stanton Harcourt was compensated with one buck in summer and one doe in winter. Our own village was of those required to drive and keep the deer for view, whenever so commanded, to "cut and make" all the grass growing in Woodstock Park and to carry it to the King's barn for the support of the deer in winter; while it was incumbent upon the not altogether to be envied owner of the Manor Place at Combe, on the occasion of a royal visit, to "clean all jakes and privies within and about the King's Manor of Woodstock.

violets, and looking around was surprised to find myself in the midst of what was obviously quite a violet-growing industry. Even the smallest cottage garden had its carefully weeded patch, while the more ambitious had spread to large plots and allotments.

I looked over a hedge and saw a small, neat, elderly, bespectacled man in tweeds and gaiters. "Come another day earlyish," said Tom Sermon, "and I'll tell you all about it." I promised I would; but the very next day, as it happened, I had to go down to Cornwall, nearly to Land's End, and it was there that I met Dick Humphreys and learnt a little about growing violets in what Sermon calls "that reddish, iron soil, that is so very good."

In Humphreys I found not only a successful nurseryman and market gardener, but a cheerful, friendly being in, I should say, his late thirties, with the Cornishman's tan and "Virginian" accent, and such a zest for his job — and for life — that all I had to do was listen while his talk bubbled over me — and try to remember a few of the lively things he said.

One thing struck me at once and that was how, when I asked him about violets, he straightway began to tell me of his pigs: the reason being of course that their manure is literally at the root of the matter. Indeed, in his view the whole secret of violet growing, provided of course you have the right soil; is first, farmyard manure — "something nice and rich for them to eat away from" — and secondly, a sheltered spot. And what could be more sheltered than those Cornish "fields," each about the size of a handkerchief, tilted to the sun and well walled with what the Cornishman calls hedges?

One of these toy fields he pointed to down by the water-mill, calling it "that field of Cheerfulness," so that I began to imagine myself in the land of Beulah and to look up and about for the Delectable Mountains. "We finished picking Cheerfulness," he told me, "on Good Friday" ("Cheerfulness" is a kind of double narcissus), and went on to talk of "the king of the trumpets," the daffodil known as "Alfred."

We walked up the steep side of the valley to his field of violets. They looked as healthy as he did himself. "Princess of Wales," he said, kneeling to explain with his hands how to deal with the runners, "you have to keep replanting if you want big flowers." But what puzzles him is the public's apparent lack of discernment. The "Princess of Wales," a large, well-scented flower, is comparatively hard to grow, and so, in the shops, just a little more expensive than "Governor Herrick," a ready spreader who smells hardly at all. Yet the public, according to Humphreys, is taking the Governor to its bosom just as willingly, if not more so, than the Princess. "They don't seem able to tell the difference," he said worriedly. (Can it really be that we are losing our sense of smell and is tobacco to blame?) He was shaking his head over this when he spied a plant with its leaves eaten by a rabbit. "Eaten his lungs," he said. But when, a row or two off, he found a fine, self-sown plant of forget-me-not, masquerading as a tall, sky-blue violet, he seemed quite pleased. "Seed must have come up on my trousers from the myosotis bed," was his comment, "a good one too."

To work two glasshouses, each with 1,400 tomato plants, four acres of early potatoes, violets, bulbs, pigs and poultry, with only one other man and a boy seemed to me pretty good going and I said so. But the restrictions, he told me, have been infinitely more onerous than the work; in particular, of course, the wartime order forbidding the growers to send flowers by post or rail. But he had "thought upon a plan": nothing less than to charter a steamer and send them by sea. Petrol, too, was *verboten*, so they hired a waggon and loaded the ship, only to find that the convoy had been delayed, and the flower ship was forbidden to sail without it. The growers were almost in despair when, after two days of waiting and wilting, a captive balloon was spotted and the convoy hove in sight. Humphreys' flowers, packed in wooden boxes, reached Liverpool still in marketable condition and sold well, though some of the others who had had to pack in cardboard, lost the lot.

Cornish violets, I learnt, are planted at the end of April or in May, according to when the right showery weather comes, and picked from October onwards, sometimes in September, but the September-picked won't usually stand up to long journeys. The plant "eases a little when cold weather comes, but doesn't stop flowering," though Humphreys owned that his valley, some two miles from the sea, gets plenty of cold winds and frost.

216

I told him of the violet growing at Stanton Harcourt, and like the eager learner he was, he showed interest at once, though he thought "as far north as that" they must grow their plants under cloches. From what I had seen I thought not, and promised to let him know.

We shook hands at the gate of the field of Cheerfulness. "My mind now is chiefly on anemones," he said.

(ii) Oxfordshire

"If it comes very severe," Tom Sermon told me, as we sat by the twinkling grate in his thatched cottage, "there's grounds for what your Cornishman said, but, take it generally, we don't suffer so bad. In fact, when we have really mildish weather there's hardly a week but what we pick, from September onwards. No, we don't use cloches, and I don't know 'Governor Herrick.' We grow 'Princess of Wales' and all sorts here."

It still seemed to me surprising that violets could be grown commercially here in Oxfordshire and in the open, without even a Cornish "hedge" to protect them; but "we're far from being up in the Derbyshire peaks, you know," Sermon reminded me and went on to refer to the weather conditions in South Oxon as "not so much worse" (according to wireless reports) as in the Channel Islands and the Scillies.

But how had it all begun? Who first had discovered that these few acres at Stanton Harcourt were so very much to the taste of *Viola odorata*? It was, Sermon told me, the squire's gardener, a man called Henwood, who had grown violets at the Lodge for Lord Harcourt and with remarkable success. "Then it was taken up by John Akers and Mark Burden. Then I come on, a matter of forty-five years ago . . . Certain villages, you know, go in for things. and it passes from one to another. And now at Oxford, yes, and even at Covent Garden and all about, people know violets can be grown as good here as anywhere."

I noticed a certain diffidence, however, when we came to Sermon's own part in building up and furthering the industry. "I saw this place had a pretty big garden," he said simply, "so I bought it and went hip and thigh in for gardening and stuck to it ever since, and here we are." But there was clearly a great deal more to it — and to him — than that. The very fact that at seventy-three — "just getting a good sensible age," as he put it — he is still an ardent student at demonstrations, as well as a successful exhibitor — suggests the pioneer, or, in Edmund Blunden's definition of "yeoman," "the kind of man who keeps the village going."

"Oh bless you yes," he chuckled, "I'm still going to their exhibitions, I'll be going this time. Oh yes, so long as I've my strength and a good bit o' land, I'll be likely to whip up and have a go."

To demonstrations, be they many miles off, he makes a point of going, "if only to learn one thing." He has small patience with the young grower who, under instruction, becomes bored and restless. "' Come on, come on,' he says and pulls at my sleeve; wants to be out and about, you know, and doing it his rough way."

218

Nor can he abide the sort who "can't tell a pea from a vetch."

I asked, of course, about prices. "It's not so long ago," he said, "if we got 2s. 6d. a dozen bunches we used to think we'd done extraordinary well. But lately I've had as much as 1s. 9d. for some twenty blooms, wholesale, and I don't know what the florists make — some extraordinary prices. But then it comes down to the time when people want something else and that evens things out. If only we could get them to bloom all through the winter . . ."

Glancing round the village, with its violet beds as neat as its thatch — and that, thanks mainly to the renowned family of Davis, is the neatest I ever saw — you might think that the flowers grew themselves. Yet snags abound. There are, of course, weeds: "Look at that groundsel, a blessed lot of rubbish gets on that. All that wants keeping down . . . Keep the plants clean and give 'em full air." There is the violet's arch enemy, red spider: "Even our expert don't hardly know what to tell you." And there is soil: "You don't want that light soil susceptible to spider, a good many have tried it and failed . . . Two miles from here they tried on stiff clay ground, but it would only grow foliage . . . On the Berkshire 'sands' they have tried it, but they can't get on."

At Stanton Harcourt there are three kinds of soil, all of which will grow violets. They are cultivated Oxford clay, gravel and a medium dark loam with light stony brash. "The best," he told me, "is a good light clay soil with this beautiful dark loam, best soil you can get for anything"; but violets will grow even on gravel soil, "so long as it's fairly rich." He "happened to know" the soil in our village was gravel, because he had been there once to get a mare. "Whip them up there if you can," he adjured me, "and tell them they grow violets well on gravel at Stanton Harcourt. Still," he admitted, "they'll grow on our ground better than in some of our adjoining villages; though I don't say they wouldn't if they persevered, that I don't know."

Like Humphreys, Sermon believes that "good decayed farm manure is the foundation of good cultivation," though he has to eke it out with a compound, and his own acre of garden bears him out. "I took this over on March 25th, 1899," he told me, "in a rather barren state . . . Now here are the early collies, and that's a little exhibition bed of onions. Here's the strawberry bed, and here's nine row of gladioli. Here are the peas" (four rows in bloom, May 25th). "This strain of pyrethrum I've had on hand over forty years . . . Sweet peas just showing colour look. Now here's violets, this is my piece, there is the wife's piece; the main bit is up at the allotment where you saw me working . . . Beans flowering well, look . . . Now this is number one tomato house — they wants water, glad I come up — you can see it's all built of home-made stuff, that latch is an old file. Built the three houses myself with a little help. Oh yes, I can lay a brick and cut glass and make a mortice and tenon good enough to carry them through all weathers . . . I'll just whip you round and then I must double back and water before getting down to some straightforward digging up at the allotment to get an appetite for dinner . . . Now here's the wife's show, a prettier show than mine. She is going in for bedding out, she can do it as well as I can. Here are the chrysanthemums, just put out . . . Here's more tomatoes . . ." and so on, plus the allotment, plus thirty head of poultry, and apples. "Last year we picked something like fifty bushels, mostly Bramleys. They seem to make wood one year and yield a good crop the next, just as well p'raps; but they look pretty good now, don't they? I don't spray. They get the poultry droppings . . ."

He admits it keeps him and his wife (his sole helper) busy, but he was brought up to it and it makes him "much happier than I would be loitering . . . It's bred in my nature. Father was a hard worker too, and no mistake, beat me at diggin' and that; but they would stick to their old stock, these old 'uns, you know, thought nothin' 'ouldn't beat it; though he had to admit in the end that with some o' this new stuff you could make an improvement."

Even our beer glasses, over the parting drink, were brought into his conversation to help make a point clear. "Now some very particular people," he said, "don't like a thick glass; but I daresay if this fell down" (picking up the thicker one), "it'd take more breaking than the thin 'un. Of course I don't know as you must pinch any glass much, but some of it's *very* frail. Now, as I was saying, take greenhouse glass. I'd rather work with twenty-ounce . . ."

And so, richer for his wisdom about greenhouses and violets and in great deal else besides, I left the seventy-three-year-old youngster, the ardent learner, and as I cycled back between green hedges and elms and fragrant bean fields, I found phrases from Cornwall as well as from Oxfordshire still running through my head. Indeed, it was almost as though one were answering the other, as in a psalm . . .

(iii) Cornwall and Oxfordshire

Oxon: A violet won't be forced. One o' they chaps tried. He only tried but once. It is a plant as enjoys its natural ways. If you think you will come tricks with it, it won't be worth your while.

Cornwall: Violets come in their season, whether lifted or not.

Oxon: Lift them against the sharp spell, lift them with a ball of soil. September is our month for lifting.

Cornwall: Violets want tickling while they grow: something nice and rich for them to eat away from.

Oxon: Good decayed farm manure is the foundation of good cultivation, but with strawy stuff you may do more harm than good.

Cornwall: The Red Spider . . .

Oxon: He is a terror, but I will tell you a good trick. Keep the yellow leaves off and so take away the harbour for the pest.

Cornwall: Our soil is very light: granite, you know.

Oxon: Our light medium is a nice drainage soil.
Violets don't want clay or sand. They
want a good medium, moderately
enriched, with a decent drainage. Get it
up and let the winter into it two months
before planting. It works so nice and
retains the moisture. That is one of the
secrets. And when you plant out, it wraps
the plant up so much nicer and it grows
away . . .

Cornwall: We grow other flowers . . . Alfred, king
of the trumpets . . . That field of
Cheerfulness . . .

Oxon: Here's the wife's show, a prettier show
than mine. She can do it as well as I can.
Her chrysanthemums . . .

Cornwall: My mind now is on anemones My son
shall grow them with sweepings from the
henhouse . . .

Oxon: I shall keep gently on a bit longer. I like to
do a thing in my quiet way . . .

CHAPTER
SIX

Nameless Stream

"THESE LITTLE MILLS"

"The only way we little men can keep going," said the miller, "is by working all hours of the day. I start at eight and I'm usually still at it when they call me in for the news at nine in the evening. To put it bluntly, it's only by making yourself a slave that it's any good to you; but here I'm my own boss, and that to me is a great thing."

We had met, my friend and I, at the door of his flour mill, a few yards from the stream, and as we talked we stood on a disused millstone let into the step. "I could tell you a good yarn about that too," he said, "how during the Plague, when the corn to feed what was left of London had to be ground at this mill . . . But no," he laughed, "I'm not sure that the mill was in existence at that time, though one expert has assured me that it quite probably was."

He went on to speak of the days of gleaning, or, as they call it here, leasing — when the mill must have been the busiest place for miles. I peered through the doorway into the dark interior, hung thickly with cobwebs like little bags and cradles of flour. The waterwheel, at that moment, was still, the whole mill empty.

It was hard to imagine the throngs of sack-laden men, women and children who must have passed through that door.

"Ordinarily," said the miller, "except for a man to hang the bags on the chain, no one enters the mill now except myself. But come and look at this . . ." and he led me to a weighing machine with, on the whitewashed wall behind it, a mass of entries in various hands, some of them recent.

"Before the village had a clinic," he explained, "they used to bring the youngsters here to be weighed. It was a great delight to the village children, a little gang of them would turn up. 'I wish you would weigh me to-day, Mr. H——,' one would say, 'I believe he is heavier than I am.'"

How dull to be weighed at a clinic when you have been used to the cogwheels and cobwebs and the floury smell of a mill! Looking more closely at the pencilled wall I made out

FATTY   10 st. 2 lbs.

"A well-known local character," chuckled the miller, "he's a grown man now, and must weigh very considerably more. No, the children don't come much now, but we still weigh our visitors. We weigh them in and we weigh them out, and if they haven't put on weight we don't consider they can have enjoyed their stay."

This from a host who, instead of extending as he was about to do when rationing came in, has had to reduce his poultry from 1,400 to about 120, and his pigs from

64 to — 5! But it is typical of his outlook, which is at once generous and mild. Hear him talk, for instance, of the milling combine and its campaign in the 1920s, for (as H. J. Massingham says) "putting the country stone-grinding mills out of action."* My friend was actually smiling as he told me he imagined the big millers saying, "We can crush them" (the little mills) "in time, as things go on," or "Leave them alone meantime to live their own life and be ousted." On the other hand, he is not so mild, this miller, as not to relish a battle of wits. "I like doing all my own bookwork, yes, I even enjoy income-tax returns," he smiled, "it brings me up against men who are better educated than I am, and I like sharpening my wits on them."

He is not a big man — the scribbled entry beside "48 lbs. Cement" reads "DADDY 9 st. 8½ lbs." — and I never can decide how much of his brushed back grey hair is white, how much merely floury.

"I took over this mill about twenty years ago," he told me, "when the bad times for farming were just beginning . . ." And so, without rancour or peevishness, he enlarged on some of what he called "the little man's troubles," from combine to balanced ration, from governmental shortsightedness to the unloading of foreign barley direct into the big plate mills at the ports. On top of it all, of course, speed; and the bald fact that, however badly they may do it, the plate mills can grind ten to forty hundredweight an hour against his almost pathetic two to three.

* "The Wisdom of the Fields," by H. J. Massingham (Collins).

"When I first started here I could manage four hundredweight," he said, "but now the place is so shaky, I have to be content with not grinding so fast. Good stuff, by the way, always goes through faster than inferior stuff."

Often enough I had seen the old mill working, but I wanted to see it again now, to see just how shaky it was. My friend obligingly began to tinker with his wedges. "It's all very simple, you know" (it looked alarmingly tricky), "you just take a wedge out of one place and put him in another, to raise it; though I suppose the modern way I should just turn a switch and that would have done the job." At last all was ready, and, while looking through a window at the stream, he raised a lever and the wheel began to turn, bringing the mill to life. Standing beside the stones themselves I was expecting to be shaken to pieces, but to my surprise the vibration was not at all excessive. In fact, I offered to show the miller a printing works in the City of London compared with which his mill is like a cloister. "A naval officer told me the other day," he said, "that it's as near like on board ship as anything."

"Except, of course, that you have flour to smell all day instead of the sea."

"Ah, but winter or summer," he said quietly, "you've only to go out of this door to see what you think is beautiful, whether it's a pear tree in leaf or a pear tree without a leaf . . ."

Yes, the setting is perfect. I like climbing to the little ivied window in the loft that looks down on to the wheel. It is all greenness.

"What is the name of your stream?" I asked.

"It has no name. It comes from the Chilterns. Two or three little streams feed it at Watlington and it runs into the Thame at Chislehampton. The Thame, of course, joins the Thames at Dorchester. I've often thought of following the stream to its source, it would be interesting."

"And how is it for supply?"

"It is a wonderfully good little stream. I used to run a mill on the Thame, you know, as well as this one, and I found this stream better, both at flood time and drought. My only trouble has been with the wheel freezing up. I've had to light straw then and faggots and keep throwing them in till the wheel began to turn."

"What are you grinding now?"

"Oh meal, always meal now. You just touch it for cows, you know, but for horses the harder it's rolled the better . . . Look at these bins" (all but one was empty), "they're for wheat, oats, barley, beans and maize . . . The shovels?" (they were ash, beautifully made), "I don't expect you'd guess what they were made for, any more than I did when I bid for them at my uncle's sale. 'You bought those two shovels, didn't you?' a man said to me afterwards, 'know what they're for? They're mud shovels, for cleaning out ponds.'* Well they suit me very nicely, when I've anything to shovel. If you don't have a wooden shovel for a wooden bin, you know, you very soon wear the bottom out."

* Mud-skuppets, each cut from one piece of wood.

It was while he was showing me a wooden, hundred-cog wheel — a wheel he had wanted to replace eighteen years ago, but the cost was prohibitive — that I noticed, hanging from a nearby nail, a much-cobwebbed leather bottle. "Yes, that was an idea too," he said, "the man whose job it was to grease the wooden cogs used to put his hand into that for grease as he went by."

"Is there much greasing and oiling to be done now?"

"Oh no, little maintenance at all. The biggest job is when a stone needs dressing. That takes all day. The 'furrows' in the stone get too narrow and the softer parts wear away, leaving the whole surface uneven. When that happens you lift the running stone up with pulleys and then you take your staff and ruddle and work your way round the stone, marking all the little bits that project. All those bits have to be tapped off with a hand-bill and you hold that in a wooden holder which we call a 'thrift.' It's quite an art. My expert at it is a bus conductor now, but he'll always come and give me a hand when I send word."

With staff and thrift and handbill he thereupon gave me a demonstration which looked slow and primitive indeed. But then of course the whole process of stone grinding is primitive and appears to have changed little since our first stream was harnessed in pre-Roman times. Indeed, according to an old book * in this miller's little office, when the Romans invaded, "the

* "History of Corn Milling," by Richard Bennett and John Elton. (Simpkin Marshall, 1899.)

watermills by which the Britons ground their corn must have created as much astonishment as the war chariots by which they mowed down their enemies." And again, "The first idea of a watermill was promulgated in Italy soon after the return of Julius Caesar from Britain."

It is, of course, only in comparatively recent years that the countryman has come to think in terms of loaves rather than flour. "People won't have flour as a gift, these days," the miller told me, "well no, perhaps that is an exaggeration; but you see I'm thinking of a gentleman of this parish who lived long ago, and, when he died, left money to provide succeeding generations of what he called 'the needy poor of the village' with a few pounds of flour."

"And the poor are no longer needy?"

"Well, that's part of it. And then people don't always like being thought of as poor and needy, you know, and their relatives like it still less. Why, only at our last Council meeting up jumps a commando with, 'Who says my Mother's poor and needy?' and goes on to tell us, very creditably, of course, that if she's short of anything, she knows who to go to." But surely, I put in, the terms of the bequest could be changed. Suppose, for instance, the money had been left to provide pattens or even horseshoes? But no, said the miller, not a word could be altered "without Act of Parliament."

Parliament, by the way, seems to take quite an interest in the mill from time to time, in the form of inspections. It was a woman inspector whom the miller, in a moment of aberration, warned about the rickety condition of the ladder — made "fast" with cord — which leads to the first floor. No sooner had he said it than he realized it was the last thing he should have pointed out to a woman whose main job was the nosing out of just such defects. However, she seemed not to have heard him as she confidently began to climb, and her next remark was, "oh, look at that unprotected shaft! You must certainly do something about that, and at once." With a smile he showed it me. It was still uncovered. "You see, I'm the only one who comes up here much," he said, "and if I kill myself, well, that's nothing to do with anyone."

It was another woman inspector, from the salvage people this time, who greeted him with, "I understand your mill is derelict, is it not? I have it on my list."

"Come inside," said the miller, "and see if you think so."

One look was enough. "The mill was absolutely bunged up with work at the time," he told me. But she still wanted to see the wheel, for it was mostly wheels she was after. The miller lifted off the bearing cap so that she could see how "nice and bright and shiny" it was beneath.

"I can see I shall have to cross you off my list," she said regretfully.

"No, we are not quite worn out," was the miller's comment.

Yet a third woman visitor — though not, fortunately, an inspector — contracted a mouse in the loft. "I looked up to see what was wrong," said the miller, "and there she was, wriggling and squealing, I should think for a couple of minutes. I didn't know what to do, so I was keeping my distance when all of a sudden, to my surprise, the mouse popped out of the top of her and scampered away. That was in my single days," he added by way of apology or perhaps explanation, "I'm a married man now and should know what to do."

I was on the verge of enquiring, as one married man to another, what the approved "first-aid" for Mouse in Clothes (Female) could be, when somehow I hesitated, and before I could frame the words he had dismissed the subject with, "It was a very uncomfortable minute or two." I don't expect I shall ever know now, but then perhaps I shall never need to.

In pre-ration days when as corn merchant, miller and expert-on-pretty-nearly-everything he used to go on his rounds, his business dealings were almost always with the woman of the house, the man being away at work. "Often you'd spend an hour discussing their affairs," he said, "but it all worked in with the business; it was mostly the local connection that kept you going. They like a local man who calls regularly, and they know what he sells is good stuff. If anything's wrong with the pig or the poultry, you're glad to give your advice. In fact, some of the things the women used to ask me . . . well, if I thought my wife told men these things I should be very annoyed."

I wondered what it all amounted to to-day in £ s. d. "On an average the mill may earn me £60 or £70 a year," he said, "yes, as I've said all along, there is not a living to be made now at these little mills alone. You must have some other line as well. I have — what's left of them — pigs and poultry, and I get my own feeding stuffs at wholesale price, that's a big advantage . . ."

We had come back to our starting-point and were standing again on the fabulous millstone. "What are those marks on the doorpost?" I wanted to know.

"Flood marks," he explained, "that one two foot up marks the time — '36 I think it was — when snow followed frost and then gave way to bright sunshine. The ground was still partly frozen and the water simply flooded back." He made a sweeping gesture to show how it had rushed into the mill. "It was bad enough then," he went on, "but before my time the mill floor was made of wooden sleepers which at flood times washed up and made a fairish old mess. Bobart had it cemented. Ever heard of Jacob Bobart who laid out the Botanic Gardens at Oxford? Well, two generations of Bobarts ran this mill. I'm only a newcomer. But we've had nothing like that trouble with flooding since the Thames Conservancy took over. They cleaned up everything, you know, did away with every weed and stick."

"How about that one over there?" I said, pointing to a stick of willow, like a fishing-rod, jutting rather prominently from the stream's near bank.

"That's for the kingfisher," he said, "and quite a favourite spot for it. I like to see them about. My son once saw five little ones being taught by their parents to fish, not far from here. 'Remember it,' I told him, 'for you won't see that again as long as you live.'"

But what, I wondered cycling home, is the secret of his happiness; for undoubtedly he is happy. Work?

Family? Faith? Independence? A balanced outlook? A bit of each, I guessed, and also because, as he told me, "I may be the exception, but to me money means absolutely nothing." And that, as I happen to know, is absolutely true.

FULL CIRCLE

It is November again, the month which four years ago saw us into this cottage, to battle with drains and chimneys and to get to know a village of which until then we had never heard.

Grouped on a little hill about the magnificent church the grey roofs looked pretty enough, but what, I wondered, was beneath them. Were the cottagers of the friendly sort we had known higher up the river, or would they be of the kind which takes pride in keeping itself to itself?

Once again we were in luck. Not only were they kind, the good neighbours who made us welcome, they were intensely interesting! One of the first to shake hands with us was Johnny Horne, the same who, fifty years before, had been hall-boy at Blenheim. I have just been to see him again and, the day being Sunday and the light wind westward, I was welcomed at the gate by the smell of Nellie's cooking which still, Johnny tells me, sends to table such stuff as dukes' dreams were made on. His parlour walls have just been distempered, and in the otherwise empty room he has hung in the place of honour a large framed photograph of a noble Edwardian, her swan-like beauty set off by clouds of white tulle and pearls.

234

"Yes, there she is," said Johnny proudly, "the dear old duchess herself."

Once again, as I looked at the torn and carefully mended photograph, I remembered and longed to write down its story; but with others it must wait. So much that is worth the telling cannot yet be told, and so much more slips quietly beyond recall every day.

Certainly it is weather for remembering. I thought so when I woke and watched the ragged horse-chestnuts grow out of the mist and heard the mistle-thrush scold from the churchyard, where it likes to keep the yew berries to itself; and I think so now this evening as jackdaws with echoing voices wheel about the spire and the robin sings his ode to autumn, his *pavane pour une feuille tombée*, which makes the time seem sadder than it is.

Now the mist is closing in again, making the sort of world in which quite ordinary people see ghosts and hear voices. I myself could have sworn I heard someone say just now, "I be glad you come. We was just thinkin' of you . . ." as Jim used when we had walked over the high words to the cottage above the Windrush.

Absurd of course, and yet it is just this sort of raw November day which puts me in mind of the Strawberry Jims, and I can see Mrs. Jim so plainly, reaching up to the cupboard for tea . . .

Perhaps it is the anniversary of the day I first went there, to be told firmly by Jim (as though I might have passed the matter by or failed to appreciate it) that my companion and sponsor was "a lovely girl." And

235

perhaps it is how Roger thought it must be, when we told him that the world was round . . .

"Then that explains," said he, "how it is that you remember things you've forgotten. It comes round to them again."

Why should the glance of love be always
The backward glance? Consider how
Time will transmute this house, these lanes, those
   woodlands —
Let them be cherished now.

FREDA BOND

ISIS publish a wide range of books in large print, from fiction to biography. Any suggestions for books you would like to see in large print or audio are always welcome. Please send to the Editorial department at:

ISIS Publishing Ltd.
7 Centremead
Osney Mead
Oxford OX2 0ES
(01865) 250 333

A full list of titles is available free of charge from:
Ulverscroft large print books

(UK)
The Green
Bradgate Road, Anstey
Leicester LE7 7FU
Tel: (0116) 236 4325

(Australia)
P.O Box 953
Crows Nest
NSW 1585
Tel: (02) 9436 2622

(USA)
1881 Ridge Road
P.O Box 1230, West Seneca,
N.Y. 14224-1230
Tel: (716) 674 4270

(Canada)
P.O Box 80038
Burlington
Ontario L7L 6B1
Tel: (905) 637 8734

(New Zealand)
P.O Box 456
Feilding
Tel: (06) 323 6828

Details of **ISIS** complete and unabridged audio books are also available from these offices. Alternatively, contact your local library for details of their collection of **ISIS** large print and unabridged audio books.

ALSO AVAILABLE . . .

No Problem
Edward Prynn

Readers of *A Boy in Hob-Nailed Boots* will know that Edward Prynn never learnt to read or write. But with the help of Jo Park he has been able to record a valuable recollection of his life in Cornwall. No Problem begins in his eighteenth year; he had left school, had several jobs, and had been delighted to find he was not fit for National Service, which meant he could stay in Cornwall, "home in the place where I belonged", with his Italian wife, Marie.

This is a man's tale about the joy of living and working, about the blows that Fate dealt him, and the problems he was able to surmount.

A Double Thread
A Childhood in Mile End — and beyond
John Gross

John Gross is the son of a Jewish doctor who practised in the East End from the 1920s through the Second World War and beyond. His parents were steeped in the customs and traditions of Eastern Europe, yet outside the home, he grew up in a very English world of comics and corner shops, sandbags and bombsites, battered school desks and addictive, dusty cinemas.

Looking back on his childhood, he traces this double inheritance. The customs that underpinned family life — Yiddish stories and jokes, the rituals and mysteries of the synagogue — is set against the life of the streets, where gangsters are heroes and patients turn up on the door-step at all hours.

Excess Baggage
Judy Astley

A funny, warm and moving novel *Sunday Mirror*

A Proper Family Holiday was the last thing that Lucy anticipated. But she could hardly turn down her parents' generous offer to take them on a once-in-a-lifetime trip to the Caribbean. As a penniless, partnerless, house-painter, with an expired lease on her flat and a twelve-year old daughter, such opportunities didn't pass by every day.

Suspecting some sinister agenda behind their parents' wish to take away, spouses, grandchildren, the lot, settle into their luxury hotel. Sunshine, swimming and good food should have melted away any family tensions but some problems simply refuse to be left at home.

Across the River
Alice Taylor

The Phelan and Conway farms stand in hostile confrontation across the river. The long dispute between the two families simmers and explodes. But the discord is not only external. Martha Phelan is locked in a stubborn battle with her son Peter. He longs to change the running of the farm but she has very different plans of her own. As the antagonism in the household mounts, it is rapidly overtaken by the force of a greater problem.

A story of land, conflict and family traditions, which captures the pulse and sinews of Irish rural life as never before.

The Wedding Group
Elizabeth Taylor

One of Elizabeth Taylor's most ambitious novels exploring the invisible ties between children and parents:

Now that her school days were over, time went slowly for Cressy. She had grown up in a world of women, presided over by her eccentric, artistic grandfather. But the wholesome values of her home life prove too restricting for Cressy and she rebels in search of more ephemeral pleasures.

Taking a job at an antiques shop, she meets David, a self-satisfied journalist, also looking to fly the family nest. But as Cressy cannot fend for herself and David is securely tied to his mother's apron strings, this act of escape for both of them proves a powerful form of bondage.

Land Girls at the Old Rectory
Irene Grimwood

A fascinating account of life at the Old Rectory, Halesworth with the Women's Land Army.

It was 1942 and Britain was running out of food. Twenty-year-old Irene Gibbs had always wanted to work on the land rather than in the cigarette factory, so she volunteered for the Women's Land Army. She and her new friends were high-spirited and adventurous. They took in their stride all kinds of farm work, encounters with farm animals and farmers, the army on manoeuvres and the US airforce, not to mention hitch-hiking, wall-climbing and some long-suffering hostel wardens.